HAL LEONARD

RECORDING METHOD

For Bands, Singer/Songwriters & More

BY JAKE JOHNSON

T0082040

PLAYBACK+

Speed • Pitch • Balance • Loop

To access audio and video visit:
www.halleonard.com/mylibrary

Enter Code
1294-4895-2098-4244

ISBN 978-1-5400-6329-8

Hal•Leonard®

Visit Hal Leonard Online at
www.halleonard.com

Contact us:
Hal Leonard
7777 West Bluemound Road
Milwaukee, WI 53213
Email: info@halleonard.com

In Europe, contact:
Hal Leonard Europe Limited
42 Wigmore Street
Marylebone, London, W1U 2RN
Email: info@halleonardeurope.com

In Australia, contact:
Hal Leonard Australia Pty. Ltd.
4 Lentara Court
Cheltenham, Victoria, 3192 Australia
Email: info@halleonard.com.au

DEDICATION

This book is dedicated to my many musical clients from around the world who have trusted me to work on their art with them. A special dedication to my partner in life, Jodie, and our amazing children, Cole and Levi, who not only tolerate me being at the studio for so many long sessions, but who fill me with love and purpose, always grounding me with what really matters in life.

CONTENTS

ABOUT THIS BOOK. 5

ABOUT THE AUDIO AND VIDEO 5

ABOUT THE AUTHOR 5

CHAPTER 1: THE PHYSICS OF SOUND. 6

CHAPTER 2: DIGITAL AUDIO BASICS 8

CHAPTER 3: BASIC GEAR AND SET-UP 13

CHAPTER 4: INPUTS AND OUTPUTS (I/O) 19

CHAPTER 5: AUDIO SOURCES. 21

CHAPTER 6: CAPTURING AND EDITING AUDIO 26

CHAPTER 7: LAYERING AND BUILDING A SONG 32

CHAPTER 8: PLUG-INS, EFFECTS, AND SIGNAL PROCESSING 35

CHAPTER 9: MIXING 41

CHAPTER 10: MASTERING. 46

ABOUT THIS BOOK

This goal of this book is to put you in the best possible position to start basic recording and production for a band or artist. In doing so, it will explore the physics of audio, digital audio concepts, signal flow, and how the basic equipment and software works. Together, we will explore how to set up your recording system, looking at microphone choices, placement for different applications, recording, editing, mixing, and mastering. In addition, you'll have access to really useful video clips to watch along the way, making concepts and techniques approachable and easy to master.

As with any topic, there is always an additional wealth of information beyond the basics that will further your knowledge and skills. But by the time you get to the end of this book, you'll have a great overview of the basics, and enough knowledge to start recording and producing music!

PROducer TIPS

Throughout this book, I will be sharing some specific tips, acquired from over 30 years of experience in recording and producing audio. These are exclusive tricks of the trade, coupled with nuggets of advice to help you get better at the craft of recording.

ABOUT THE AUDIO AND VIDEO

This book includes online access to audio tracks and video tutorials, for download or streaming. Simply visit **www.halleonard.com/mylibrary** and enter the code from page 1 of this book. Icons are used throughout the book to indicate where specific audio tracks or videos apply to the lessons.

ABOUT THE AUTHOR

Jake Johnson is the senior producer, engineer, and owner of Paradyme Productions, an award-winning recording studio and production facility in Madison, Wisconsin. Jake has been nominated for multiple Emmy awards for his audio work and has won multiple accolades including Producer of the Year, Studio Engineer of the Year, numerous Albums of the Year, and dozens of Songs of the Year awards in genres spanning rock, hip-hop, country, R&B, pop, and folk.

After starting in the 1980s recording onto analog tape, Jake was a part of the digital revolution, doing beta-testing for companies designing audio software and updating systems every few years to keep up with the rapidly changing technology. Since then, he has engineering and production credits on over 500 nationally released albums and over 3000 songs for hundreds of different clients. A voting member of the National Academy of Recording Arts & Sciences (the Grammys), Jake is also a frequent panelist at music conferences across the country and has taught and mentored many students through academic recording programs. He is the author of multiple books about recording, technology, engineering, and production.

CHAPTER 1: THE PHYSICS OF SOUND

WHAT IS SOUND?

We all know that our ears hear sounds and that there are a variety of different sounds. There are *high-frequency* sounds like birds chirping, *low-frequency* sounds like a bass drum, loud sounds like fireworks, and quiet sounds like whispers and breathing. We can make sounds in various ways, such as using our voice, striking an object, plucking a string, or even rubbing our hands together. Sounds are simply vibrations that travel through the air. Our ears pick up these vibrations and our brain converts them into signals we can interpret and understand. Even with our eyes closed we can hear passing cars, dogs barking in the distance, and even the wind in the trees.

Let's look at a simple video to illustrate how sound travels through the air.

DRUM HIT SOUND WAVES

When a drum is struck, the impact with the drum moves the head (top membrane) and causes the entire drum to vibrate. The air around the drum is made up of molecules—tiny particles of nitrogen, oxygen, carbon dioxide, and hydrogen—all with space between them. The vibration of the drum creates ripples in the air near the drum, compressing air molecules together and creating spaces between other molecules. These ripples then travel outward from the drum as the air molecules bump into other molecules and create a wave of high- and low-pressure zones. When these ripples enter your ear canals, your eardrums sense the pressure differences, converting them into movement and a signal your brain understands as sound.

Figure 1
A snare drum being struck by a drumstick. The picture on the left is the initial impact. Then, as the movement of the drumhead causes the drum shell to vibrate, the vibration causes ripples in the air that travel outward from the drum in all directions. These areas of high and low pressure within the air are what we refer to as *sound waves*. These sound waves decrease as they spread out, which is why it is loudest near the drum and quieter as you get further away.

The sense of hearing is vital for everyday life, from communicating to navigating and making sense of the world around us. It is also important in making entertaining music. Music is the manipulation of sounds and audio signals to bring about emotion. Next, we'll look at the basic ways that we capture and reproduce this sound.

HOW A MICROPHONE WORKS

A microphone is a device that captures the vibrations in the air and converts them into a voltage that can be transmitted by a wire (or wirelessly) so that sound can be amplified or recorded. As with your eardrum, the microphone has a thin diaphragm that moves in and out in response to sound pressure waves that are hitting it.

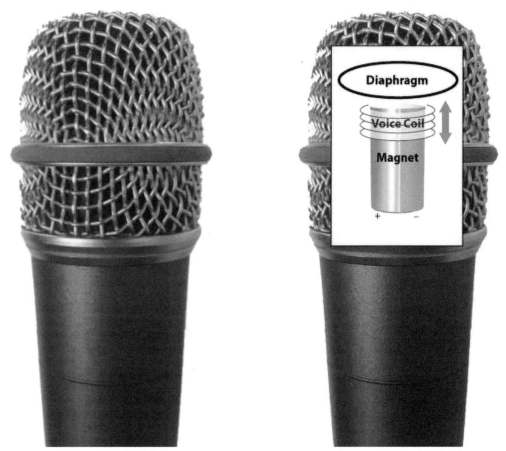

Figure 2
A dynamic microphone with a cutaway, showing the sound-capturing mechanics.

In a basic dynamic microphone, illustrated in Figure 2, the diaphragm is attached to a coil. Sound pressure waves hitting the diaphragm push it inward and pull it outward in response to changes in air pressure. Inside this coil is a magnet, and as the coil moves in and out, the magnet creates an electrical voltage. That voltage is then transmitted into a wire, changing the sound pressure waves into an electric signal. This changing electric signal, or flux of voltage, can then be recorded or amplified.

HOW A SPEAKER WORKS

A speaker is simply a device designed to reproduce pressure waves in response to an electric signal. To put it more simply, think of it as a microphone in reverse! Based on a fluctuating voltage in the wire that feeds into the speaker, a large magnet inside the speaker pushes and pulls the speakers outward and inward, creating air pressure waves that travel through the air. The speaker pushes and pulls the air molecules in response to this electronic voltage flux, and those pressure waves enter our ears.

CHAPTER 2: DIGITAL AUDIO BASICS

When you are working on audio on a computer or other electronic device, you are working with *digital audio*. Instead of the sound signal being stored as a fluctuating electric charge, like in the past with magnetic tape, modern audio is stored as a digital code on a hard drive or as stored media on the cloud. This code can be played, reproduced, manipulated, and output without introducing unnecessary noise—which can be common when working with electrical circuits. It is mathematical, and as a result can be duplicated, transmitted, and stored flawlessly.

With rare exceptions, almost all music that is recorded today is stored and manipulated digitally. In the past, audio was recorded onto records using a groove and a needle, or onto tape using magnetized particles to capture and reproduce an audio signal. Storing the information that makes up the audio waveform digitally gives us countless tools with which we can edit, combine, process, and shape audio without the limitations of storage media, or the purchase and maintenance of expensive specialty analog hardware with moving parts. The advantages over older methods are multiple, including less noise, easier storage and transfer, no signal loss over time, perfect synchronization between multiple audio and/or video sources, and easy editing and digital processing via software. In the same way that digital photography changed how we take and process pictures, digital audio technology has revolutionized how we work with recordings and music.

DIGITAL WAVEFORM

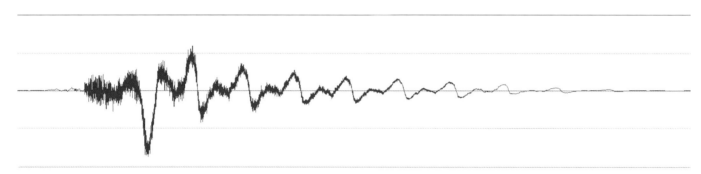

Figure 3
A complex digital *waveform*. The horizontal line represents the speaker at rest with no sound. For simplicity, let's call this center line the "zero line." In digital audio, it represents "negative infinity," or the lack of audio. The waveforms above this line occur when the speaker is pushing out towards you, and the waveforms below this line happen when the speaker is pulling away from you. Together, this signal represents the sound that was recorded. Note that this waveform contains low and high frequencies shown together, with the low frequencies represented by the wider curves in the waveform and the high frequencies indicated by the quicker up-down curves within this larger curve. This waveform depicts a drum hit in which the high frequencies and the loudest part of the hit occur right at the point of attack. It then tapers off in volume over time. The bright crack of the stick hitting the drum is evident in the prevalence of high frequencies at the beginning. As the sound is decaying with time, the high frequencies decay more rapidly, with the sustain of the drum hit being mostly low frequencies.

FILE FORMATS

Digital files and waveforms can be saved in many different file formats. The most common are mp3 files, wav files, and aif files. As with digital photos, there are different qualities or resolutions for files. Smaller files are easier to transfer and download but typically are of a lower *fidelity* or quality.

Wav files and *aif* files are lossless files. They tend to be large—containing lots of information and storing high-resolution audio. They are used in digital audio recording, mixing, and mastering. *Mp3* files are a compressed format that sacrifices some audio quality for a smaller size and quicker access. The lower the *kbps* (kilobytes per second) value, the smaller the space the data is packed into, and thus, the lower the quality. Mp3 files with higher kbps values will be larger in size, but generally will sound better due to increased resolution.

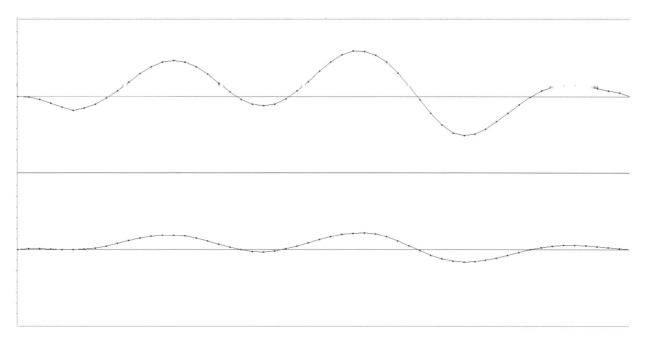

Figure 4
A close-up view of a complex digital waveform showing the individual samples, or data points. This is a stereo waveform, with synchronized but separate data for the left speaker (top) and the right speaker (bottom). Note how the waveform on each side is simply the connection of these individual data points.

SAMPLE RATE AND BIT DEPTH ▶

The *resolution* (or fidelity) of your digital audio signal is dependent upon two main factors. The first is *sample rate*, or the number of samples per second of audio, represented horizontally on the digital waveform (X axis). The second factor is the *bit depth*, which is the amplitude resolution of the sound data that is captured and stored in an audio file. This is represented vertically on the digital waveform (Y axis).

Let's use a video analogy to help understand these two factors better. In video, the more individual frames (or pictures) you take every second, the crisper and smoother the video will be. This is because the differences between each picture are minimal, producing a smooth, flowing, moving picture when viewed together. The more choices for colors and the number of pixels within each picture in the video, the higher the resolution will be and the crisper your images will look in every single picture along the way. Sample rate is akin to the number of frames per second in a video, and bit depth is akin to the number of pixels or resolution in each picture.

In capturing and recording audio, the more *samples* (or "snapshots") you take every second, the better you will represent the audio you are capturing. Similarly, the more values you have for amplitude, the more accurately that snapshot will be represented and connected to adjacent snapshots. Low sample rates will miss out on some high treble frequencies that can't be represented, and low bit depths will result in unwanted additional noise and an inability to accurately capture quiet sounds.

CD-quality audio is 44.1 kHz (sample rate measured in *kilohertz*) and 16-bit (*bit depth*). This is a significantly higher quality than anything you can hear on the radio, from your phone, or streaming from the internet. It is possible to record much higher sample rates and bit depths than CD quality, and they will be bigger files with greater resolution. This sample rate of 44.1 kHz, or 44,100 samples per second, will let you capture frequencies just over 22 kHz, which is higher than most adults can even hear.

While sample rate is linear (88.2 kHz is literally double the number of samples as 44.1 kHz), bit depth is exponential. That is to say, 17-bit audio gives you *double* the resolution of 16-bit. 24-bit audio is 256 times the amplitude resolution of 16-bit audio.

MONO AND STEREO

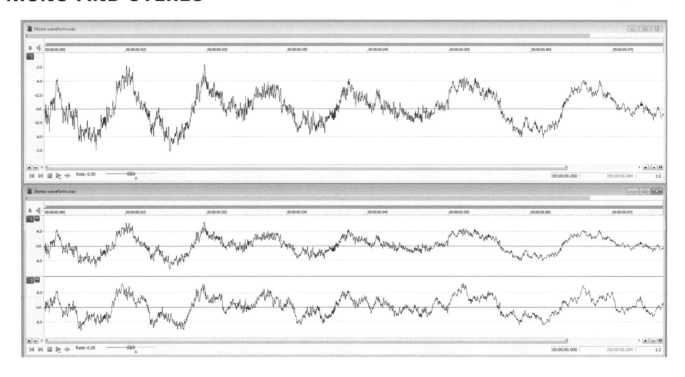

Figure 5
The top image shows a *mono* wav file, with a single channel of information. The bottom image shows a *stereo* wav file, with two channels of information. Note how the two channels of the stereo file look a little different. This is because they contain different data, with some audio shared between the two channels, and some audio unique to each channel.

Simply put, a *mono* sound is a single channel sound, and a *stereo* sound has two channels. When played on a two-speaker stereo system, a mono file will play the same sound out of both speakers. Conversely, the stereo file will play one channel out of the left speaker and the other channel out of the right speaker. By having differences between the two channels in the stereo file, our ears receive different signals, and our brain consequently perceives that we are in a three-dimensional space.

HEARING IN STEREO ▶

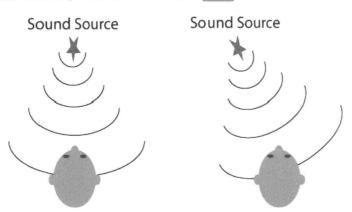

Figure 6
Hearing in stereo (*binaural* hearing). The left illustration shows a sound signal directly in front of the listener. The sound waves hit both ears at the same time with equal power, and the listener's brain tells them the sound came from straight ahead. The right illustration shows a sound signal in front and a little to the left of the listener. In this case, the signal entering the listener's left ear will be slightly earlier and slightly louder than the signal entering their right ear. The difference in timing and power of these sound waves as they hit both ears is processed by the listener's brain, telling them that the sound source is a little to the left and in front of them.

We have two ears that are constantly hearing different signals, telling us not only what sounds we are hearing, but also the direction and distance of those sounds. If a sound is coming from one direction, it enters both ears at different times and with differing power. Our brain can detect these minute differences in timing and tonality.

When working with music, keep in mind the stereo field in which we hear sound and use it to your advantage. We'll elaborate on this more in Chapter 9 when we cover mixing. For now, note the differences between mono files, stereo files, and waveforms. Begin to think about music in three dimensions, and how we can spread out different elements within this stereo field to help paint an audio picture.

PROducer TIP: When to Record in Stereo

Stereo files take up twice as much storage space as mono files. When you have a single source, like a single microphone or line signal, record a mono file. When you have a stereo source, like a pair of microphones on a choir or stereo outputs from a keyboard, record a stereo file. This way you will capture the additional stereo components of those sounds and make your recording more dimensional and interesting. Recording a stereo file of a single mono source is just wasting hard drive space and gives you no sonic benefit. The signal on the left will be identical to the signal on the right, so your signal will still be mono despite the file being stereo!

DAWs (DIGITAL AUDIO WORKSTATIONS)

Digital audio workstations (or *DAWs*) are essentially software packages for recording and processing music. We use them to capture, edit, arrange, process, mix, and master audio. Some DAWs have hardware components built into them that you can add to the software. Others are just software that you use on your computer. There are many DAW options in the market. Commonly used packages include Ableton Live, Logic Pro, Pro Tools, Cubase, FL Studio, Studio One, and Reason.

PROducer TIP: Match the Software to Your Audio Needs

I often get asked, "Which DAW should I use?" My reply is usually a question, "What do you want to do with it?"

There are several DAWs designed for beginners. These are usually easier to use but a little less powerful and with fewer professional capabilities. They may only support a few file types but are more affordable and readily available online. There are also DAWs designed for professionals that have greater functionality and power. However, these can also be quite expensive and potentially very confusing for the beginner. My advice is start with an easier DAW and master it. The first guitar I ever owned was a cheap, used, no-name guitar. Once I got better at playing and realized the limitations of my entry-level instrument, I upgraded to a new, mid-level guitar with a floating tremolo that worked great for the '80s music I was into at the time. Years later, I went with a slick, classic guitar model that I still play today. Like a guitar, think of your DAW as a tool. Once your skills and requirements become restrained by your DAW's limitations, upgrade to a professional package with the functionality you need.

In addition, you should choose the best DAW for your specific requirements. If you are arranging music and need to work with MIDI and print sheet music, you will likely be using a different DAW than an engineer who wants to record and mix live bands. Some DAWs are designed for specialist usages, such as for producing electronic music or for working with audio and video combined. I have used dozens of different DAWs over the years depending on the particular situation. Oh, and don't forget to check that your computer and operating system can actually support the given software *before* you buy it!

Most DAWs feature an editor window, a mixer window, and a transport window. In an *editor window*, you can visually see the waveforms and tracks, and you can manipulate the takes. In a *mixer window*, you can apply effects and leveling to all of the audio on each track. In a *transport window*, you can play, record, stop, rewind, loop, and control the playback. In entry-level software, you might find that these features are combined into a single window.

The editor is useful for picking your preferred takes, moving parts in time, applying fade-ins and fade-outs, and muting or removing parts of takes you don't want to use. In the following image, note the ruler on top showing where you are in time within the song. This ruler can be set to "minutes and seconds" or to "bars and beats"—which would show you the measure number and beat within that measure.

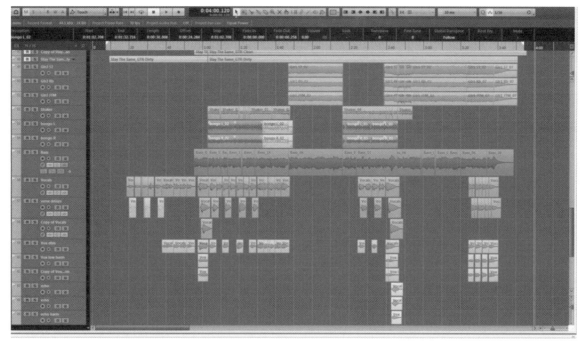

Figure 7a

A DAW's editor window. From the editor window, you can see the different tracks and takes within those tracks. Each horizontal row is a track containing parts of one voice, or one instrument source. The horizontal axis represents time, so the left side of the window is the beginning of the song, and the right side is the end of the song. The "now line" (cursor) will move to the right as you play the song, playing the combination of the parts recorded. Using color and labeling is a helpful way of making the editor window easier to use and navigate. Zooming in on individual waveforms can help with fine tuning takes or combining different takes into a part.

The mixer is useful for leveling tracks against each other, applying *EQ* (equalization), *compression* (see Chapter 8), or effects to tracks, and for sub-grouping audio tracks together. We will dive deeper into using the mixer and its various components in Chapter 9.

The transport window allows you to jump to different sections of the song, enables functions including record, play, stop, loop playback, and even allows you to set the area you want to hear or record into. Most DAWs assign the space bar as a start/stop button for easy use as well.

Figure 7b

A DAW's mixer window and transport window. The large window taking up most of the screen here is the mixer, with each track representing one of the columns. These columns correspond to the rows of tracks in the editor. In addition to leveling each instrument on its track, you can apply EQ and effects to each track separately to customize the sound on each separate track. You can mute (M) or solo (S) individual tracks, or combinations of tracks, to help you home in on the sound you want. The small window in the upper right is the transport, with buttons for forward, backward, stop, play, record, and more. In professional DAWs, you can customize these windows to best suit your particular needs.

CHAPTER 3: BASIC GEAR AND SET-UP

EQUIPMENT AND HARDWARE NEEDS

The first thing to think about when you are deciding what gear you will need is what you'll be recording. Most people think about vocals, but will you also be recording guitar or piano? Maybe some drums or other percussion? Will it be a solo act playing one thing at a time or will it be an ensemble with multiple musicians playing and singing at the same time? What is the maximum number of inputs you will need at any given time? Think about all of what you will want to capture and plan your gear needs based on that.

Figure 8
The picture on the left shows a singer recording on a single microphone, singing along to previously recorded guitars, and using only one input. The center picture shows a singer who is also playing acoustic guitar and recording both vocals and guitar at the same time, using two inputs. The right picture shows a guitarist playing her guitar parts using three inputs, which include two microphones in stereo on the guitar and a *DI* (direct input) coming from her guitar's internal pick-up.

Figure 9
Drum microphone inputs. Placing a microphone on each drum in a drum set gives you more control over the sound of each piece and more flexibility in the mix, but it uses a lot of inputs. The simplified set-up on the left uses seven inputs (kick, snare, two tom-toms, hi-hat, and a pair of overhead mics capturing cymbals and the whole drum set), while the more detailed set-up on the right uses 17 (with a mic on every drum and every cymbal, plus a pair of overhead mics and a pair of room mics).

BASIC RECORDING GEAR

For the most basic set-up, you will need a microphone, a preamp, a sound card, a computer equipped with a DAW, and monitor speakers. The microphone will capture the sound of an instrument and/or voice. That signal will feed into the preamp where you will amplify and level it, and possibly apply some EQ or compression. The signal will then go from the preamp into the sound card, where it is converted into digital audio and made usable by your computer, which outputs sound to the monitors or speakers, allowing you to hear it.

Keep in mind that you will also need microphone stands, microphone and speaker cables, and microphone clips. You'll also need acoustical treatments to get your recording space sounding better before you start recording. We will cover types of microphones and their uses in more detail in Chapter 5.

Preamps

A *preamp* is a device used to amplify a microphone or line signal. Preamps will let you adjust the level going into your system and many will also allow you to add EQ, compression, or overdrive to generate the sound you want out of your device. Preamps are the devices that take signals from the microphones and lines and get them ready to record. They can be all shapes and sizes, and some sound cards include channels with built-in preamps. Most mixing boards have preamps on every channel. The maximum number of inputs you will be recording at any given time will determine the number of channels you will need preamps for. For a vocalist singing into a single microphone, you will only need a single preamp. For a band recording live all at the same time, you may need 24 different inputs and 24 channels of preamps. We'll cover more on using a preamp in Chapter 6.

Sound Cards

The *sound card* is the audio converter in your set-up. Signals come from microphones and lines into preamps. The processed signals come out of the preamps and feed into your sound card. The sound card converts the signals from analog voltage into digital signals for your computer so these digital signals can be recorded into your DAW. There are many brands and types of sound cards. The number of inputs on your sound card should be equal to or greater than the maximum number of input signals you will be recording at one time. Many sound cards will come with software that displays an interface for the card that you can see and manipulate on your screen.

PROducer TIP: Picking a Sound Card

Sound cards vary hugely in both cost and quality. Good quality analog/digital converters are a component of professional sound cards that help to capture a truer sound with less noise. Professional sound cards featuring these converters understandably cost more. If you will be simply playing ukulele and singing, a small and easy-to-use sound card is all you will need. You can get a basic two-input sound card with built-in preamps for $100. For basic home recordings and getting your song ideas recorded, an inexpensive sound card might be adequate. As you step up to higher-quality preamps and more inputs, the price goes up accordingly.

If you want to record clean voice-over material or achieve a professional recording quality for your band, go for a professional-level sound card. Check your computer and the specs on the sound card to make sure they will be compatible. Ensure that any sound card you get has the adequate number of input channels for your recording needs.

ACOUSTIC TREATMENTS

We've all noticed how sound in different spaces can vary drastically. Think of how your voice sounds in a carpeted library full of books versus a gymnasium, or how sound carries inside of a tunnel compared to inside of your car. How different does a room sound and feel when you take the furniture and rugs out of it?

For most applications, the space you record in should not be overly prone to echoes and reflections. Think of how an empty stone church sounds. It may produce a flattering musical soundscape for a choir, but diction can become very difficult. It's hard to understand someone who is talking in a space such as this because there is a long reverberation caused by reflections of the sound off surfaces in the space. Everything you would record in that space would have that thick reverb on it, so you would be limited in your ability to shape the sound. Most modern recording spaces have a number of acoustic treatments, which can be divided into two basic types: *absorptive* and *reflective*.

Absorptive Materials

Materials made to absorb sound pressure waves that are placed in strategic spots can drastically reduce the reflections in the room and allow the engineer to control the sound they are capturing. You can always add more reverb to a signal during mixing, but taking reverb away is a much trickier job. Keep in mind *all* of the surfaces in a room, including the ceiling and floor, and remember that padded furniture is itself a very absorptive material that can really help the sound of any space for recording.

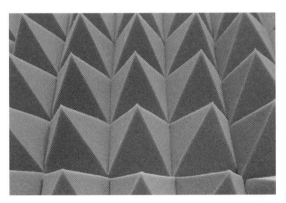

Figure 10
Some examples of acoustic treatments to control reflections in a room. The picture on the left is a foam product you can put on walls and ceilings. It is made in various thicknesses to absorb a wider range of frequencies. The middle picture is a compressed fiberglass panel. These soak up a lot of sound off of flat surfaces, preventing sonic reflection back into the room, but these particular panels are heavier than the foam products and require different mounting techniques. The picture on the right is a rug and carpeting. A nice carpet or rug can really help absorb sound reflections within a room and reduce the noise from feet on a hard floor as well.

A space with acoustic treatments and controlled reflections also has a better response to varying distance from a microphone. As a result, the sound captured is more consistent throughout a take when the performer is moving, whether they are strumming a guitar or bowing a violin. You will notice you have better control over sounds, and you will hear less bleed into other microphones in a room if your space contains absorptive material.

Reflective Materials

Walls, flat flooring, and windows are all very reflective. They become a problem when the room is too reflective or reflective surfaces are parallel to each other, creating bad spots within the room due to accumulation of certain frequencies or standing waves. Materials made to reflect and scatter sound pressure waves from flat and/or parallel surfaces can make your room more suitable for recording. If you can't afford to build new walls that aren't parallel with each other, using *diffusers* to scatter sound in multiple directions is a good idea.

 To understand this, think of the way that light responds to mirrors. Shining a bright light on a single flat mirror would produce a beam of blinding light wherever that mirror faced. Now imagine shining a bright light on a disco ball, covered in tiny mirrors. In this case, tiny spots of light would be spread around the room. Diffusers are like this for sound—scattering reflections so that you don't get a concentration in one area of a room.

Figure 11

Pictured above are some examples of diffusers used to scatter the sound reflections within a space, often placed on flat surfaces. They cause sound waves to reflect at different angles and at different times. The picture on the left is a plastic molded diffuser, and the picture on the right is a wooden diffuser designed to both absorb and deflect sound at different angles and distances.

Isolation

In most cases, you don't want outside noises like traffic on your recordings, so you need good walls, doors, and windows to provide good isolation from those outside sounds. What we think about less is the need to keep sounds recorded in one room, isolated from the sounds in adjacent rooms. For example, when you have a singer in a sound booth, you don't want the sounds of speakers in the adjacent control room to get onto their vocal track. Most studios have specialty walls that are thicker and designed so that sound doesn't pass through them. Foam and carpet help reduce reflections within a room, but do very little for isolation, or keeping the sounds from escaping the room. Heavy materials and using building techniques to isolate walls from transferring vibration are the key to good sonic isolation.

If you have multiple performers using the same room to record in at the same time, like a horn section, finding ways to give them a little isolation from each other will give you a better recording with more flexibility down the line. When you don't have the space to put each performer in a different room, using physical dividers or large panels to separate the space sonically will give you better isolation on your tracks. Cubicle dividers and large panels work well to help divide a space into smaller, more isolated recording units. They also help cut down on reflections in the room.

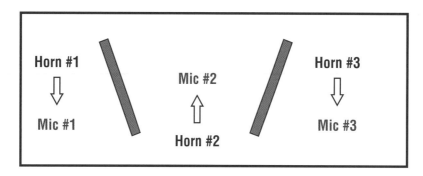

Figure 12

A large rectangular room is subdivided using cubicle panels to achieve better isolation for each of three horn parts being recorded at the same time, and to help break up the sound reflections in the room. The result will be three signals with less bleed from the other horn parts, allowing you to have more EQ and leveling control, with easier editing.

Using microphones that are directional in nature (with *hyper-cardioid* or *super-cardioid patterns*) will also help you with isolation. A tighter pattern on a microphone means it will pick up less of the sounds on the sides of the mic and more of the direct sounds coming into the front.

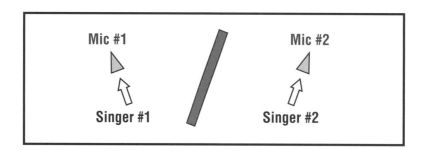

Figure 13

The same large rectangular room, but now it is subdivided for two vocalists using a cubicle panel. Using a tighter pattern on the microphones allows each singer better isolation on their track, as the microphones they are singing into will pick up less sound from the sides.

SIGNAL PATH

Understanding the *signal path* (where the audio signal is travelling) and what is happening along that circuit is crucial. Let's look at an example.

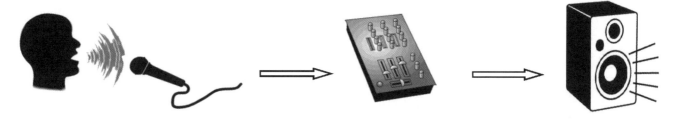

Figure 14
A simple signal path starting with a vocalist singing into a microphone, through a mixer, and ending with output from a powered speaker.

A singer's vocal cords vibrate and create pressure waves in the air, which are picked up by the microphone. The microphone responds to the vibrations it picks up and converts those pressure waves into a voltage that is transmitted through the microphone cable to a preamp in a sound mixer. The preamp is used to bring up the level of the signal into the mixer. Within that mixer, the tone and level can be adjusted, and effects can be added to manipulate the sound. The newly processed audio signal is sent out to an amplifier built into the speaker. This pumps up the voltage so it can move the speaker in and out to create new pressure waves in the air, producing new processed sound for the audience to hear. In this case, the signal path is rather simple and linear. You can follow it from the source (the person) to the final output (the speaker).

Now imagine a whole band, consisting of many different performers and instruments, all being recorded independently with multiple microphones to be later combined and mixed to produce a well-blended sound. Each instrument will likely have EQ and effects that are separate from the other instruments. There may be more or fewer components within each chain. For example, the guitarist might be playing their guitar through a distortion pedal into an amplifier on stage, which is then picked up using a microphone on the amplifier that feeds into the mixer. The drummer most likely has multiple microphones on different parts of the drum set, which are each EQ'd and effected separately to get the desired sound out of each drum and cymbal. Those signals are mixed together and sub-grouped into a single overall drum signal, to be mixed in with the rest of the band. The singer is likely in a different room for isolation, using a condenser microphone and running into a different preamp. The rest of the band will want to hear the vocals in their headphones, so it will need to feed into the headphone mixers for every musician. Each recorded instrument will need to feed into the headphone mixers as well, so the singer can follow along with the rest of the band.

The more inputs and variables, the more complex a recording set-up can be. Understanding the signal path of whatever set-up you are using is critical to being a good sound engineer. It is also crucial to effectively tracking down problems when they arise.

PROducer TIP: Write It Down!

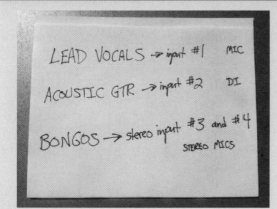

Make a simple chart or spreadsheet to keep track of your inputs and where they are routed. Knowing where each signal is coming from and its path is essential in recording. It will help you during a complex recording session to quickly make level adjustments and track down noises or missing audio signals. Staying organized and having this map will allow you to control and capture the best sound possible while staying on top of things during a busy recording session.

DIFFERENT RECORDING SET-UPS FOR DIFFERENT SITUATIONS

Most people imagine a musician going into a studio and being recorded in exactly the way that they would perform live. This is what is referred to as *live recording*. The performer or performers play the song live as if it were a show, with all the parts being recorded together. Each instrument has a line out or a microphone, and the recording engineer brings in all of the different signals on different channels so each part can be manipulated later to achieve the best sound during mixing. They may perform each song a few times and pick the best one, or use pieces of each take to combine into a single, solid performance.

Figure 15

This guitar duo is rehearsing their parts before they record them together live. If the performers are well rehearsed, live recording can be a quick process that can help capture the raw, live energy of performing in the moment.

Another common method of recording is multi-tracking. This is sometimes referred to as *overdubbing*, because in the days of analog tape, you could add (or "dub") new parts to existing recordings by recording them onto (or over) the same tape. In *multi-tracking*, each performer plays at different times, so you can clean up takes from each instrument and get the most out of each take as you are going. For example, a band might wrap up recording the drums before moving on to recording bass and, later, recording guitars. This tends to be easier for the engineer, as there are less variables to focus on at one time, and it is easier to detect mistakes. Recordings made this way tend to be tighter in timing, and parts contain less *bleed*—meaning there are no other instruments being played at the same time whose sound might be escaping into the part you are recording. Therefore, each track is cleaner and can be manipulated independently.

Although you get increased flexibility and ability to tighten things up, you will likely spend more time recording this way. Some musicians argue that they lose the connection with other musicians when multi-tracking on their own, and others love how they can perfect their individual parts. The most suitable method of recording (or indeed, a hybrid of the two) will be determined by your preferences and desired outcome. If you want your recording to sound like a live performance with the personality of a concert, track it live (also, mic up the audience to capture that spontaneous energy). If you want it to sound tight with each element perfected, use overdubbing and multi-tracking.

Figure 16

This bassist is playing his parts along with pre-recorded drum tracks. The vocalist sang through the song and recorded a practice vocal track, or *scratch track*, along with a metronome click track. This technique allows all other performers to know where they are in the song as they are playing their parts. The scratch vocal track will be replaced later with a final vocal take and harmony vocals once all of the instruments have been recorded and edited. In this case, the drummer played his parts against the scratch track and metronome, and those takes were cleaned up for timing before the bassist started laying down his bass parts on the song.

CHAPTER 4: INPUTS AND OUTPUTS (I/O)

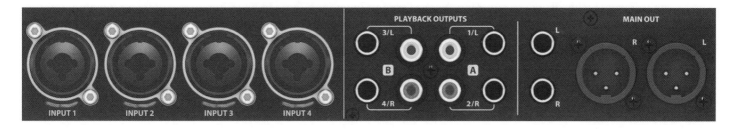

To put it simply, your *I/O* (*input/output*) set-up is how you get sound into and out of your computer. In your DAW, you will need to set up your I/O so that your software recognizes your sound card and sees all of the inputs and outputs that you will be using. Many computers have internal sound cards as well, but for any music application, use your separate audio sound card as that will likely provide much better sound quality and access to all of your inputs and outputs. The I/Os on your sound card are numbered and the software uses this numbering to determine which input to record, and which output to send the signal to. If your sound card came with software, you will likely be able to use the software to mute I/Os and adjust the volume coming in or going out for performers, so they have the right mix in their headphones.

MANAGING INPUTS AND RECORDING

Your inputs will be available in your software so you can record the various signals patched in from your mixing board or preamps. For the track you are recording, your DAW will capture and record whatever is coming into the selected input for that channel.

For example, if you are recording vocals and piano, you may have the piano's stereo microphone going through a stereo preamp and into inputs #1 and #2 on the sound card, and the vocal microphone going through a preamp and into input #3 on your sound card. In your DAW, you would set up two tracks: the first for the stereo piano signal, and the second for the mono vocal signal. On the piano track, you would set up a stereo input using inputs #1 and #2. On the vocal track, go to the inputs and select the mono input #3. Then, once you've armed those tracks and hit "Record," you will be recording everything coming into inputs 1–3, with the stereo piano signal going to the stereo piano track, and the vocal signal going to the vocal track.

OUTPUTS

In a basic set-up, you would use only the main stereo audio output as the only output. Everything coming out of the DAW would be directed to outputs #1 and #2 on your sound card, which would be sent to your active speakers or the power amplifier powering your passive speakers. This way, you have a left signal coming out of your DAW into your left speaker, and a right signal coming out of the DAW to your right speaker.

In a more complex set-up, you might utilize outputs with a satellite system so that different performers playing at the same time can adjust their headphone mixes. Or you might set up an output to send a pre-recorded guitar signal to a tube amplifier. This will allow you to change the sound using a real guitar amplifier. Similarly, you can send a pre-recorded audio signal out to external effects and processing.

BUSSES

Busses are simply signal paths. They can be used to combine or route signals within your DAW. The one bus that everyone uses and is familiar with is the *main output bus*. Your DAW has a mixer that combines the various signals that you record and sends them all to this main output bus so the whole mix can be played on your two speakers.

You may want to set up a sub-group bus within your DAW. This will allow you, for example, to send all of the drum and percussion tracks to a sub-group where you can apply compression or effects to all of the drums at the same time. Another example is to combine all of the backing vocal parts into a single sub-group, where you could use a de-esser and/or compression to easily control volume with a single fader. Sub-groups can make mixing easier and can free up power for your processor by using less plug-ins (covered in Chapter 8).

Busses can also be used to split a signal to multiple places. This can create what's called a *side-chain* for signal processing—splitting different instruments to different outputs on your sound card.

CHAPTER 5: AUDIO SOURCES

START AT THE SOURCE

Audio can come from a singer, a drum, a guitar, an amplifier, the output of a keyboard, or any other sound you want to record. Before you start thinking about which microphone to use or which input to set up, think about your source and how you can get it sounding as good as possible. The beginner often fails by skipping the basics of getting a good sound.

For example, when considering a vocalist, ensure they are comfortable and have water to drink, that their voice is warmed up, and that they are hearing a good headphone mix (which means they can clearly hear themselves while singing). Much like an athlete preparing for a race, preparation, warm up, and hydration is the key to a good performance. For a guitar, check that the instrument has good strings and is in tune. If there are any effects in the chain, make sure they aren't too extreme for the song. It's easy to add more effects later, but difficult to take an effect out of a recorded guitar part. For a drum set, make sure the drums have new heads on them. The head types should match for each drum. You don't want one bright drum that sustains and one warmer, dead drum that doesn't. Make sure that a hit cymbal won't come in contact with a drum or a stand and that the pedals don't squeak. Check the tuning on the drums and ensure that the cymbals aren't clamped down so tight that they sound deadened.

One basic method to follow is to go through your chain systematically and make sure each instrument sounds good first. No amount of processing will make up for a singer that isn't warmed up, an out-of-tune guitar, or a squeaky kick drum pedal.

MICROPHONE SELECTION

Picking the right microphone and choosing the right settings can help you capture a good sound from your source. While there are no hard-and-fast rules, there are some microphones that are designed to work better with certain sources, or in certain recording situations. Check the frequency response and pattern(s) on microphones you are considering to make sure they are right for the situation.

Dynamic vs. Condenser Microphones

In general, *dynamic microphones* work better for recording loud signals with high *SPLs* (sound pressure levels), like snare drums and guitar amplifiers. *Condenser microphones* work better for capturing quieter signals and sources containing high frequencies such as vocals, violins, mandolins, and acoustic guitars. Most of this has to do with the basic microphone design. Dynamic microphones are typically more rugged and more directional than condensers. They also do not need phantom power from the preamp to operate. Condensers are a newer technology. They can capture a truer sound in a wider pattern than most dynamic microphones and have a charge stored on their element. As a result, they need *phantom power* (DC electric power, +48V) from the preamp to operate. You'll see a switch on the preamp to turn phantom power on and off. The main drawbacks with condensers are that they tend to be more expensive, can be delicate and costly to repair, and their larger *diaphragms* (the sensitive components in microphone capsules that vibrate in response to sound waves) can distort easily at high SPLs.

Figure 17
The picture on the left is a commonly used dynamic microphone. The picture on the right is a commonly used condenser microphone. The condenser has a larger diaphragm and captures a truer sound but has drawbacks as well. Each is used in different situations based on their specific advantages and disadvantages.

ACOUSTIC INSTRUMENTS

Acoustic instruments sound great using a condenser microphone. Condensers capture the bright details and bring a true sound to the recording. For acoustic guitars, ukuleles, and other similar instruments, placing a condenser microphone about halfway up the neck, angled in toward the body of the instrument, gives it a nice, crisp sound. Pointing a microphone toward the body of the instrument and away from the strumming hand will result in a more hollow, woody sound. If you are able, place a pair of condenser microphones in these two positions and pan them out in stereo. The resulting recording will sound like you are sitting right in front of the instrument. This helps to provide a subtle stereo image, encouraging vocals and other center-panned sounds to pop out more.

PROducer TIP: Avoid the Sound Hole

Many beginners make the mistake of placing a microphone right on an instrument's sound hole. The *sound hole* helps an acoustic instrument project its sound and be louder, but the sound heard directly in front of the sound hole tends to be "muddy" and "woofy," and doesn't include the delicate highs generated by the strings of the instrument. Yes, it is loud in front of the sound hole, but the tone is much more pleasing and easier to control when the microphone is not placed directly in front of it.

I often notice that a player will rotate their instrument after the mic has been set up, moving the sound hole in front of the microphone. Remind the performers where you've placed the microphone, and ask them to stay in that relative position so the tone of their instrument doesn't change throughout the take (see "Finding the 'Sweet Spot'" at the end of this chapter).

AMPLIFIERS

For many instruments, like electric guitars, electric bass, lap steel, and crunchy blues harmonica, the desired sound is achieved by running the signal through an amplifier and putting a microphone on the speaker of the amplifier to capture that sound. In addition to providing amplification, an amplifier helps shape the sound. Placing a dynamic microphone near and toward the center of the speaker will capture the most bass.

Figure 18
In the left photo, a dynamic microphone is placed in the center of an amplifier's speaker. Moving the microphone outward from the center towards the edge of the speaker, or angling it off axis, will reduce low-end frequencies and feature more mid-range frequencies. In the right photo, a dynamic microphone is pointed toward one of the four speakers in a 4 x 12 speaker cabinet, plus a condenser microphone is placed three feet off the speaker as an *ambient microphone*, capturing more of the room sound.

As noted earlier, get the instrument sounding good first, then plug in the amplifier and dial in the desired gain, EQ, and effects. Once you are happy with that, place a dynamic microphone on the speaker and test the sound coming through. Make any adjustments, bearing in mind that the output of the instrument will impact what is going into the amplifier, so you may need to adjust that as well. For distorted guitars, make sure the amplifier is outputting enough volume to break up the signal, giving you an appropriate amount of "crunch." Then, adjust your preamp so you have a good recording level and aren't sending a signal that is too hot into your sound card. As a general rule, if the sound through the amplifier is improved, then use it. If the amplifier doesn't help or it adds a bunch of noise that you can't control, then go without it or try a different model.

PROducer TIP: Fatten Up Your Tones!

If the sound you are getting out of your amplifier is too thin, try adding bass from the instrument and then the amplifier if necessary. Experiment with the amount of gain and cutting or boosting frequencies on the amplifier. A tube amplifier will give you a nice, warm gain, so I always recommend using one if you can. Larger speakers and closed-back speaker cabinets tend to produce more low-end frequencies, so try some different amplifiers and speaker cabinets if you are able. If the sound is still too thin, check that the microphone is as close as you can get to the center of the speaker and try cutting the high frequencies on your preamp. Or, as a last resort, you can EQ the track after it has been recorded. The earlier in the chain you can improve the sound, the better your end result will be, and the more flexibility you will have in mixing.

LINE INSTRUMENTS

For a keyboard, sampler, electric violin, electric guitar signal coming out of a digital processor, or electric bass guitar, you may want the unaltered sound to remain as pure as possible without "coloring" it through an amplifier. In this case, use a *DI box* (direct injection box). Using an instrument cable, plug the instrument into a DI box. Then, use a microphone cable to get a nice, loud signal going out of the DI box into your preamp. Remember, for stereo instruments like a keyboard or workstation, you will need two DIs, or a stereo DI. Otherwise, you are only getting a mono side of your stereo signal. Some preamps will have a line input on them as well; you can bypass the DI and plug straight into the line input(s) on the preamp(s). Use your preamp(s) to adjust and level signals that are coming into the sound card. In the case of a stereo signal, make sure you have similar settings on your two preamps so you hear compatible signals on the left and right.

SPECIALTY SOUNDS

A unique microphone or microphone technique can help you get a unique sound. One common technique is using a close and distant microphone on the same source. The close microphone will be dryer and more direct. The distant microphone will capture more of the room reverberations, sounding diffuse and distant. You can blend those two signals to get the desired sound.

Some old microphones or specialty microphones have an idiosyncratic sound to them that can help add character to your recordings. For instance, to sound like an old-time recording, some folk artists will use old RCA microphones, as featured in recordings from over 100 years ago. They can be fun to work with but be prepared for some noise and sonic limitations.

Similarly, *ribbon microphones* can provide a nice, warm sound since they are bad at capturing high frequencies. Be careful though, because along with this feature is a fragile element that is susceptible to breaking in wind, or when used on loud sources. This microphone picks up signals from the back almost as much as it does from the front.

I worked a session with a singer who wanted his vocals to sound like he was in the galley of a wooden ship. Rather than renting a ship to record on, we built a long wooden box out of plywood that was open on the two ends—essentially, a rectangular tube. After recording his vocals on a close microphone, I sent that dry signal out through a separate sound card output and into a small, clean, guitar amplifier that I placed on one end of the long wooden box. I then put a condenser microphone on the other side of the box. We combined this "reamped" signal (run through the wooden tube) with the close microphone signal to get a sound that truly captured the character of a small wooden space. It worked beautifully, and his vocals sounded like he was in a wooden ship hull!

I found another fun technique at our studios in Madison, WI, where I put the performer on the middle landing of a stairwell and placed a microphone one flight down from them in *omni-directional mode* (picking up sound with equal gain from all sides or directions). I then placed another microphone one flight up from them in omni mode, panning the two microphones left and right to create an intense natural reverb from the stairwell space. Combined with a close *cardioid microphone* (typically a heart-shaped pick-up pattern) directly on the performer and panned down the middle, I could control the amount of reverb by turning up and down the stereo-split microphones.

It can be a lot of fun to experiment and try some new ideas to create some new sounds.

PLOSIVES AND POP FILTERS

I prefer to have a singer close to the microphone to capture the full character of the voice. You can get a nice, crisp sound using a condenser microphone equipped with a *pop screen* (or *pop filter*). This screen will help diffuse the puffs of air created when a vocalist sings a "P," "B," or "T" sound. Without the pop filter, that puff of air will be interpreted by the microphone as a big, low-frequency blast. These *plosives* can severely interfere with your vocal performances and recordings.

Figure 19
The pop filter pictured here stops puffs of air from hitting the delicate diaphragm of this condenser microphone. Note how it is placed just inches away.

MIC PLACEMENT

For a violin, placing a cardioid condenser microphone 12–18 inches over the instrument and facing down at an angle provides a good sound and gives the performer room for bowing without hitting the microphone. In the picture on the left, I have both a ribbon microphone and a large diaphragm condenser microphone on the violin in the same relative position. I blend the low frequencies from the ribbon microphone along with the brightness of the condenser to get a full violin sound. In the background, notice that I used this same technique on the banjo in the adjacent room as well.

For a mandolin or ukulele, place a condenser pretty close to the strings where the neck meets the body, but angled toward the middle of the instrument. The proximity will give you a nice, rich sound, but again, be aware of the performer and their movements.

For an upright bass or cello, try placing a condenser microphone 6–8 inches off the *bridge* (the piece of carved wood that supports the strings and transmits their vibrations to the belly of the instrument). A good volume can be captured there, and the frequencies are more balanced and even compared to the region around the *f-holes*, which emphasize certain tones more than others. These holes are f-shaped cuts in the belly of the instrument, which enhance its volume and tone overall, but much like the acoustic guitar, the tone heard at the sound holes is not a fully balanced tone and tends to be "boomy."

For percussion and drums, placing the microphone on the top will provide the most crispness, while the inside of the drum will give you greater resonance and the least bleed. Try both methods to find what works best for your situation.

You could also try a blend. Keep in mind that if you have two microphones facing opposite directions on the same source, you will likely need to flip or invert the phasing on one of them so they can be used together. This prevents both microphones working against each other in response to the same pressure waves, as one is pushed in while the other is being pulled out. This is a simple way of inverting your signal and can be done easily on most preamps or in your DAW. You'll notice the sound improvement immediately once you flip the phase on the preamp for one of the microphones. Your signal will be both fuller and louder when the phases of the two signals match.

Room and distance microphones can be a fun way to capture the sound of a space. But keep in mind that the mic's isolation will decrease the farther away it is placed. In a room with two guitarists and a drummer, the guitar microphones will surely pick up some of the drums, so moving the microphones close to the guitars or amplifiers will lessen the amount of drum bleed on the guitar tracks. Likewise, positioning guitar amplifiers in a different room than the drum set will not only help isolate the guitar sounds but will make for a cleaner drum sound too. Again, keep in mind that using microphones with narrower or tighter patterns pointed directly at the source will cut down on bleed from the room as well.

PROducer TIP: Finding the "Sweet Spot"

I use a very simple technique for microphone placement that has proven to be useful and effective time and time again. Have the musician play their instrument as they would during a performance. Ask them to play normally. Cover one ear with your hand and face your other ear at their instrument. Get nice and close. Then move around. Where do you like the sound of the instrument? What angle and distance is the most pleasing sound coming from? Remember that position and try putting your microphone there. It's so simple and such a good way to sonically explore an instrument—to hear where the "sweet spot" is and mic it. Maybe try finding a couple of spots that you like. Try putting a microphone on both and see what you get. Once your microphone(s) have been placed where you like the sound, remind the performer to not move around too much so that you can capture a consistent sound throughout their takes. Adjust positioning and levels as needed, and if using two microphones, try panning them out in stereo for a nice effect.

CHAPTER 6: CAPTURING AND EDITING AUDIO

Now that we've covered some of the basics on how to get the best sounds coming into your DAW, let's go over recording and editing. Recording is the act of capturing waveforms and editing is the act of manipulating those waveforms within your software.

- Open up your DAW and editor window.

- Add a track to your editor.

- Check your inputs and ensure they are configured.

- Set the input on the track to the source of your signal.

- *Arm* your track. This is usually done by clicking the red circle on the track you created. This tells your software that when you click the record button, it will record any signal coming into the designated input on that track.

- Do a few test recordings, adjusting the input level on your preamp as required.

RECORDING LEVELS

The level at which you record a signal into your DAW is independent of the level it will be in your mix because you can change that later. What you'll want from the start is a good recorded signal that doesn't *clip*, or go past *digital zero* (the loudest sound your software can record). On the other end, you'll want a signal that is recorded with enough level to be manageable while avoiding the noise associated with a low-level signal. Too quiet a signal means you will need to gain it up later, which will also result in turning up noise. An ideal recording level avoids clips from loud signals and avoids excess noise from quiet signals.

HEADROOM

Headroom is the amount of potential space you are allowing above your signal as a safety margin in case something loud happens on the track. In general, give yourself 3–6 dB of headroom on a track (dB = *decibels*). Aim for something that peaks around -6 dB at the loudest point, so if it goes a little over -6 dB, you have room to spare before it clips. Recording meters in your software will help guide you to where the *peaks* (loudest parts of a take) are. The visual waveforms created by the software will give you a gauge on which direction to adjust the levels. If you see the meters clip (hit red), attenuate the signal coming into the sound card until you see no more clips on the loudest parts. If it is barely showing up in your DAW, chances are you'll need to have the instrument or amplifier louder, or you'll need to gain-up the input on your preamp.

PROducer TIP: Finding Optimal Recording Levels

Setting recording levels is a bit of a fluid process. Use the performer's warm-up take as the time to watch and adjust levels. You never know when a performer might inject more energy into a take or hit a big, climactic part of the song where the levels will increase, so allowing some headroom is good preparation for such a scenario. For a song that is very emotional and dynamic, give a little more headroom than you might at first be inclined. It will save you from having to do the whole track over with adjusted levels.

Keep in mind that, if you are recording at 24-bit, you don't need to be as worried about having the levels so "hot." This is because you will still have good resolution at low levels, so you can afford a little more headroom. Once you have a good recording level, with the performer where they need to be, you can adjust their headphone level so they have the right mix while performing.

PREAMPS – INPUT GAIN VS. OUTPUT LEVEL

When using a preamp or mixing board, you will often see a dial for input gain and a separate dial or slider for output level. *Input gain* is to bring the level up coming into your preamp. For a crunchy tube sound, turn this up to drive the input tube harder. The *output level* is then what you would use to attenuate the signal to get a good recording level. Keep in mind that any EQ or compression in your chain will affect these levels too. For instance, if you have a good level and then boost the treble or the input gain, you will also be boosting the level going into your sound card. This means you'll need to, once again, check your recording level and adjust the output level as needed.

SEGMENTS AND TAKES

Each time you record to a track and then hit "Stop," you have created a *take*. A take is represented visually with a waveform on the track you have just recorded onto. Most DAWs will allow you to record multiple takes on top of each other, with the most recent take being the one you hear (shown on top). If you move or remove the top take, then the previous take will play. People often use takes when they have a hard section of a song that they want to try multiple times. Then they can pick through the takes to find the best one or compile a single version from fragments of multiple takes.

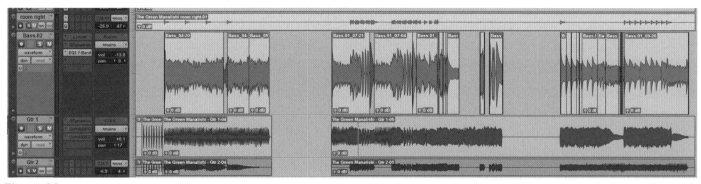

Figure 20
Here is a bass track. It was recorded in pieces and edited so you can see multiple segments from multiple takes. Some parts were moved to be in time with the song. Other parts were punch recorded to replace mistakes (more on this in the next section). Together, these segments make up the bass track for the song. Below the bass track are two separate guitar tracks recorded in two takes with minimal editing. Each track can be comprised of multiple segments. The segments will play in time as they are arranged within the track.

PUNCH RECORDING

Often, a performer will do a few takes and decide on the one that they would like to use for most of the track. There will usually be a few spots that they could do better or want to deliver differently. Any modern DAW will allow you to record a small replacement section on a track, and this is called a *punch-in*. There are a few different ways you can do this, but the easiest to understand is this:

- Find the best take overall. Make It the active take on your track.

- Using your *split tool* (often depicted as a scissors in your DAW), trim out the section you want to replace. The best choices for splits are between words or phrases, where a new take coming in will be imperceptible.

- Using the selection tool, select and delete the section you wish to replace (it will disappear from your screen but is still accessible as a remaining part of the original take).

- Make sure that the track you are working on is armed for recording.

- Let the performer(s) know where you will be punching in and start playback a few lines before this spot so they can sing or play along. This is important so that the performer(s) can enter with the appropriate timing, tempo, and character at the punch-in.

- Hit "Play," and as the section approaches and the performer is singing or playing along, hit the record button on the transport.

- Once they are past the end of the punch section, and you are at a good breaking point for the performer, press "Stop."

- Use your selection tool to drag the starts and ends of the take to a good spot to cover the punch-in area and overlap the edges with the previous takes.

- Cross-fade the punch-in segment with those segments around it as needed.

- Play back to check that the replacement take sounds good and is sonically compatible within the track.

- Repeat as needed until you record the punch take you like.

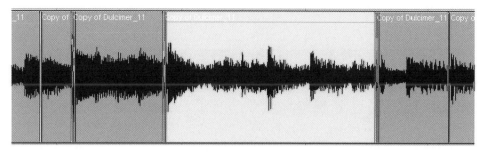

Figure 21a
The picture above shows a single take with some editing. The section to be removed and re-recorded is the light colored segment of take #11.

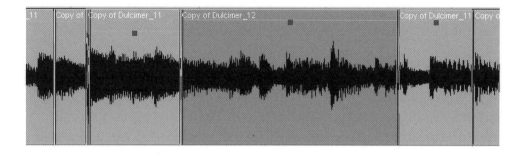

Figure 21b
This picture shows the new punch-in (take #12) placed in the track where the old segment was removed. Once the cross-fades are applied (more on this in the following section), the new take blends in with the old, making a new-and-improved track. This new track sounds like a single, uninterrupted unit, with the edits undetectable to the listener.

PROducer TIP: Punch More Than You Need

In some cases, there is a temptation to punch just one word or a tiny part of a take. Keep in mind that when you record over one take with another, you still have both takes to use. I like punching in a line a little early, and likewise, punching out a little later than is actually required. The advantage in doing this is that you will have multiple choices of where to place the *cross-fade* (transition) from one take to the next, because you have a lot of overlapping material. Also, humans are not perfect, and timing, volume, energy, and expression may be different between takes. Having more recorded material than you need will give you more options for the punch-in. Sometimes, a performer delivers a new take with something that is preferable to the older take anyway. For instance, if you've got material in excess of the amount you actually needed to re-record, then using that new extended take is now an option for you too. Remember, you can always use less than the full content you recorded within a take, but you can't extend a take beyond where you recorded.

EDITING

Editing is a broad term that can include making tiny adjustments to timing and pitch to rearranging and processing entire sections of the song. Some basic editing that you will almost always have to do includes simply cleaning up beginnings and endings of takes with *fade-ins* and *fade-outs*. This helps remove unwanted pops or extraneous noises from the starts and ends of takes. Additional editing functions that are common include:

- Removing sections of takes where the instrument isn't playing.

- Turning down unwanted noises, loud breaths, or squeaks.

- Replacing sections by using punch recording or copying and pasting.

- Moving sections in time to tighten up the take with the other tracks.

- Adding or moving cross-fades between takes.

- Compiling pieces of different takes into a single take.

CROSS-FADES

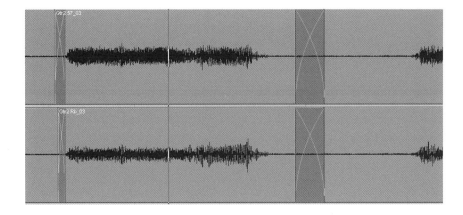

Figure 22a

A *cross-fade* describes the moment when one track fades out while another track is fading in. It is used to make transitions smooth between takes or segments. If done right, the transitions are undetectable to the listener. Within these tracks above you can see a short cross-fade on the left, and a longer cross-fade on the right. Note how the cross-fades occur in breaks during the take. Cross-fading when an instrument is not playing is much easier and smoother than cross-fading while an instrument is playing.

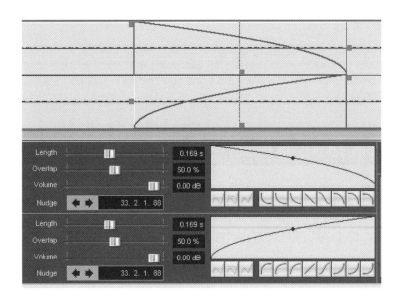

Figure 22b

Above is another depiction of a cross-fade between two recorded segments. This shows that you can set the fade-out and fade-in type for each segment, the length and the shape of the fades, and how quickly each fade occurs.

SPLITTING

Use your split tool, or *trim tool* (scissors), to remove unwanted sections or to tidy up takes that contain long sections of unwanted material recorded at the beginning and/or end. If you select a group of tracks using your selection tool (e.g., all of the drum tracks within a take), your split tool will split all selected segments at the same split point in time. Remember, this is all *non-destructive editing*, so if you cut in the wrong place, you can simply undo it and cut again. Alternatively, you can just move your cut to the correct position. Most DAWs have keyboard shortcuts to functions like splitting and cross-fading.

COMPILING

The act of *compiling* (*comping*) a track is simply picking your preferred parts from multiple takes and placing them all on a single track. When recording this way, the performer can run through the whole song multiple times without interruption, which some prefer.

Once you have a few good options to comb through, listen to each take and use color to code the sections in terms of quality. This makes it much easier to visually compile the good takes together onto a single track. Keep in mind that you may still need to go back and punch-in any difficult spots.

MOVING, COPYING, AND PASTING ▶️

Sometimes it works well to use a good take of a repeated riff or chorus and copy it to another location in the song. This is simple to do, especially if you recorded to a metronome. It is useful if you want to duplicate a favorite version of a repeated section of music or to eliminate repetitive editing and clean up work.

- Find the section you want to copy. If need be, place splits along the edge and select the segments that correspond to the source tracks for your copy so that only the section you want to use is copied.

- Select all the segments you want to copy/paste and copy this selection.

- Pick the destination time for your paste, keeping in mind that the selection you copied will paste from the earliest segment in time. If you are using bars and beats or grid mode, it can be very easy to select your destination based on the starting position of the source material.

- If misaligned, move the pasted segments into place.

- Cross-fade this newly pasted section with adjacent segments as needed.

PROducer TIP: Organize Your Tracks and Takes

As your projects get bigger and more complex, it will become increasingly important to work in an organized way. The names of audio files you record in your DAW are automatically derived from the track title you are recording them into, so label your tracks *before* you start recording. This simple task also keeps you from accidentally changing settings on the wrong track, because the track name appears in both the editor and mixer.

Organize your tracks in an order that makes sense to you. I like to put drums together in a specific order (left to right from the drummer's perspective), followed by percussion parts and bass parts. This way the rhythm section is grouped together on the mixer, allowing me to edit it as a whole when fixing timing and adjusting the volumes and EQ of individual microphones within the drum set. I also use color to differentiate parts of the song or different instruments. Bright yellow works well for highlighting spots in the editor window that need replacing or fixing. Sometimes, a performer wants to record multiple takes and compile a final take later. In this scenario, I label takes in chronological order and make notes on each track as I hear parts I really like. I then create a new track labeled "Comped Vocal" or "Comped Guitar," into which I drag segments while compiling the takes. This way I can easily see parts that I liked, as well as those that need fixing or replacing. Once I'm confident I have the comped take I want, I delete the segments I did not use right away. This keeps things clean and my hard drive space well-managed.

Try doing some test recordings. Sing or play along with your recordings to match them up. Try putting in another track and clapping along. Practice punching-in and splitting/editing audio. The more you get a feel for the tools and how to make adjustments, the better you will be at learning the next steps. This is the path to becoming a recording engineer. After working for many hours within your DAW, you will find little tricks to become more efficient and skilled. Put in the hours to do repeated tasks, but also to experiment. All of this will make you a more solid and well-rounded engineer.

CHAPTER 7: LAYERING AND BUILDING A SONG

ADDING LAYERS

When creating a song, it is important to understand that additional depth and width will make it more interesting to the listener. Think beyond the basic layers of a live performance. What would a second guitarist play, or what would an additional singer sing? The answer to this can be as simple as doubling up on parts or recording additional tracks with different strum patterns or voicings. Layering can also be achieved by adding tones from different instruments or amplifiers and adding percussion or harmonies. The additions don't need to be complex to be effective.

To illustrate some ideas on how to effectively use simple layering, listen to the song "Free Fallin'" by Tom Petty. As you listen to the intro, note how the initial guitar part actually comprises two separate 12-string guitars playing the same strum pattern in stereo, with one take panned *hard left* and the other panned *hard right* (meaning the signal is sent exclusively to the left or right speaker, respectively). There is also a bright electric guitar panned right that is playing high voicings of the same chords up the neck, adding a crisp, chiming guitar part to help make the sound interesting and thicker. The use of these three simple guitar parts creates a cool stereo sound and leaves plenty of room in the center for the lead vocal, which on entry can be heard clearly without being too loud because it has its own space in the stereo spectrum.

Listening on, note how simply adding in the bass and drums gives an energetic lift as verse 1 transitions to verse 2. Observe how the sound changes when it hits the chorus. The acoustic 12-string guitars basically play the same part as the verse but with extra energy and a little more strumming. The obvious change on the chorus is the vocals jumping up an octave with a nice delay effect added. Less obvious is the change in the bass and electric guitar parts. Can you hear the bass sliding more on the lower strings, and the electric guitar now playing the lower strings while mimicking the bass slides? All of this provides a little more depth, which, combined with the change to the vocals, helps to both lift and differentiate the chorus. We now have a fuller sonic picture, with greater width and depth achieved by filling in the low-mid frequencies when the vocal jumps up to hit the high leads. These are all simple layering additions, but they are consciously done to induce mood, a sense of structure, and a sonically interesting three-chord song.

PROducer TIP: Add for the Choruses, Take Away for the Verses

Making room is a very simple way to give energy to your songs. All too often, band members feel the need to play their parts for the whole song. A band with two guitarists may have them both playing parts for the entire song, front to back. I've often heard the comment, "This is how I've always played it live." Here's my advice: You are in the studio now. Don't you want to sound *better* than you do live?

1. Take something away for the verses. By taking out one of the guitar parts, simplifying it, or even changing it to a piano or a thinner acoustic part, you are creating room to grow. If you start out at 100%, it's pretty hard to boost to a new level of energy when you hit that big chorus. The solution can be as simple as going with a lower-gain, cleaner sound for the verses, and saving the gain boost for the choruses. Another idea is to just double all of the guitar parts, and then take away one of those parts during the verses.

2. Add something in for the choruses. Think in stereo. Maybe it's taking a single strummed guitar part and doubling it up. Maybe it's adding tones, like an electric guitar on top of some acoustic guitars. Maybe it involves doubling up the vocals, adding some simple harmonies, or applying a nice effect to give the vocal more of the spotlight. Maybe it's adding a percussion part, like a shaker or tambourine. Maybe it's a combination of a few of these ideas to help push those choruses to a new place sonically and energetically.

Using these simple ideas can take recordings to a whole new level, while staying true to the songs and the musical stylings of the artist. Production ideas during tracking often end up making it into the final mix, but you don't always have to use them. Try some new layers and experiment, but don't forget to take elements away in your mix to create space where it is needed.

USING MULTIPLE TAKES, ALTERNATIVE RHYTHMS, AND VOICINGS

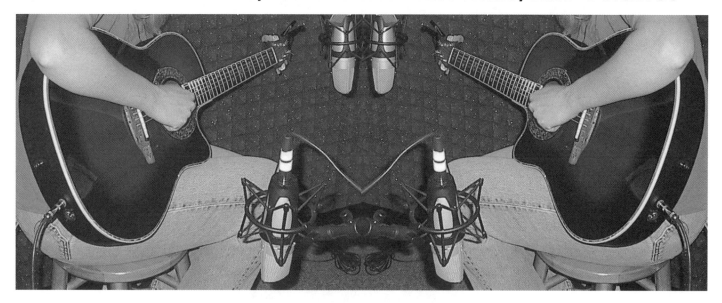

One of the simplest things you can do to add production value to your recordings is to double-up your tracks by performing the same take twice on different tracks. Subtle differences in timing, energy, and pitch will add new dimensions to a recording and thicken up your take without having to re-invent a new part or employ supplementary instruments. Often a *doubled track* can help widen a sound and make the volume and energy more consistent as well. Try panning out those takes to different parts of the stereo field.

Doubling a part on another instrument or through a different amplifier can also be a simple way of adding depth. Besides doubling, think about where the song could use an alternate rhythm for greater impact. One easy thing to do on a section that needs more energy is to add either guitar strums or piano chords on the changes. In addition, by letting those chords hang and sustain (as opposed to adopting the rhythmic patterns of the rhythm section), we avoid taking up room that the vocals require, and we're not adding strum patterns that might prove distracting.

Voicings are the combinations of notes that make up chords. For most instruments, there are multiple voicings available for each possible chord. By adding chords with alternative voicings, you are not only creating variation in timbre and tone quality, but you are likely getting a few different octaves of notes than your original voicing.

Listen to the song "Mercy" by Shawn Mendes. The intro and first half of verse 1 feature a simple, low-pitched piano part and solo vocal over a four-chord progression. Halfway through verse 1, Mendes lifts up his vocal melody and doubles the piano chords with a clean electric guitar, adding some finger picking for variety. After the big chorus, in verse 2, the piano reverts to its role from verse 1, but the guitar is now rhythmically altered and a busier acoustic guitar played with palm muting is heard. Halfway through verse 2, a higher, sustained keyboard is added, playing different voicings of the piano's chords, emphasizing only some of the notes. This thickens out the texture to build towards the chorus. A simple "ooh" vocal is also added to provide further layering between the low piano and high organ.

Remaining within the confines of the same four chords, these additional layers combine multiple rhythms and varied voicings to generate a nice build, giving a simple harmonic progression sonic interest and movement. Note also how the drums and "choral" vocal harmonies are the big additions to the choruses, while their absence in the verses provides for maximum impact and structural variety.

PANNING AND 3D THINKING

In a two-speaker stereo field, the *panner* determines how much of the signal from a track goes to the left or right speaker/headphone. You can pan a sound all the way to one speaker or the other, or you can put it at any ratio between the two speakers. Good recordings utilize this spatial positioning to provide separation and clarity to the individual parts. The technique also adds sonic interest by exploiting how our brain processes the differences between the signals going into each of our ears.

Panning allows a recording engineer to give definition to two parts that are occupying similar frequency ranges. Let's take, for example, a folk song that has an acoustic guitar, a bass, and a celtic harp.

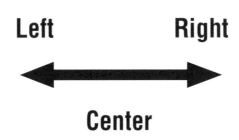

Left   **Right**

Center

Panning the guitar and harp parts a little bit outward to each speaker allows each instrument to occupy its own space. This means each one can be more clearly differentiated while still featuring in the same overall listening space. Since the bass is occupying a different frequency range, it can be *center-panned* (down the middle), grounding both sides of the stereo spectrum with common low tones. An engineer can experiment with different amounts of panning to find what feels right. Even subtle panning, tilting right or left, can help widen a mix and get clarity out of each instrument in the ensemble.

In addition to panning, effects can be used to place a performance into a specific setting. Use of time-based effects like reverb and delay (see Chapter 8) can really add depth and a sense of open space to a track. Adding a medium-room reverb can make the studio-recorded folk band sound like they are performing together in a small venue. Remember, you are painting a picture with audio, so take care to be sensitive. When dealing with reverb and delay, a little can go a long way.

Listen to the vocal effects at the end of the song "Shining Star" by Earth, Wind & Fire. The vocal part for the last line goes from the sound of a big, spacious hallway to a completely dry effect without any reverb. When I listen to this, it makes me feel as if the singers were up on a stage performing in a large concert hall in front of me and then, suddenly, singing directly into each ear. The panning spread between the vocal harmonies provides clarity, an effect made more extreme by taking out the stereo reverb. This combination of panning and effects illustrates how reverb and special positioning can create the perception of a performing space, or ambience. It all combines to make the sounds on a recording more interesting and stimulating.

CHAPTER 8: PLUG-INS, EFFECTS, AND SIGNAL PROCESSING

WET VS. DRY

When someone says that they would like to hear the track "dry," this means without effects. A track with effects on it is said to be "wet." A track loaded with a bunch of effects is often referred to as "too wet" or "overly effected." As with anything in art, sometimes a very intense effect is desirable, and sometimes it can be annoying or distracting. Using effects in an artistic way (both *when* and *how much*) is often the sign of a mature engineer. Most plug-ins have a wet/dry balance built into them. This is often labeled as "mix" with a slider that can be set from 0% to 100%, so you can manipulate how much of the effect is used. As for how wet to make your track, so much depends on your style and preferences. Listen to some of your favorite songs critically. Try to hear what effects are used, how much they are used, and when they change.

PLUG-INS AND EFFECTS

Audio *plug-ins* are software programs that add functionality to your DAW. They have their own interface that you can configure and tweak. The effect can be added as you wish to tracks or can be used to process segments in your DAW. There are literally thousands of plug-ins made by dozens of companies that do a wide variety of processes. Here are some of the most common ones.

Time-Based Effects

- *Delay*. A copy of the audio is repeated back at a set time or distance from the original audio. Delay effects are sometimes called *echo* or *slapback*. Typically, you can manipulate the timing of the delay, whether it repeats, and for how long. You can set it to match the song tempo or a subdivision of that tempo.

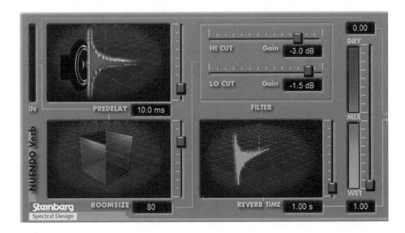

- *Reverb*. Short for *reverberation*, or the sound of reflections within a space. A reverb effect plug-in will add ambience to a track, making it sound as if it is in an echo chamber, hallway, or room. In actuality, this effect is simply a series of delays that decay slowly and overlap. Typically, you can manipulate how intense the reverb is, how long the signal lasts, and other characteristics like the EQ of the reverb sound.

Listen to the following audio examples of a snare drum, both dry and processed. The processed examples utilize different time-based effects with alternate settings.

 Track 1 – Snare Drum, dry

Track 2 – Snare Drum, short reverb

Track 3 – Snare Drum, long reverb

Track 4 – Snare Drum, delay (300 ms, 30% feedback)

Track 5 – Snare Drum, delay (94 ms, 0% feedback)

Frequency-Based Effects

- *Modulation.* This bends the pitch of a signal up and down at a steady rate. It can have an intense impact and can be used to create many other effects. Typically, you can manipulate the depth and speed of the pitch bend.

- *Chorus.* This is an effect that mixes a subtle, delayed modulation signal with a dry signal to create a sound similar to doubling. By blending in a slightly pitched and delayed version of a take, the chorus effect creates the digital impression of multiple performers. A stereo chorus uses different modulation in each side of the stereo spectrum, creating a spacey stereo effect. When used heavily with more modulation depth, a chorus can give an "underwater" sound to a track.

- *Flanger.* This effect is basically a chorus but using a much smaller delay and a tiny bit of modulation. This processed signal is then looped back on top of itself (*feedback*). The sweeping EQ shift is enhanced in a flanger effect compared to a chorus, and feeding it back generates a whole new sound impression.

- *Phaser.* Also called a *phase shifter*, this effect is created by shifting the original audio slowly in time, and then recombining it with the dry track. In doing so, some frequencies are accentuated, and some frequencies become phased out. As the timing of the shift changes, a phaser impression is created, like a sweeping EQ effect. Typical parameters that can be tweaked include the depth of the phase shift, the speed of the time shift, and the intensity of the effect.

Listen to the following audio examples of a vocal, both dry and processed, utilizing different frequency-based effects.

 Track 6 – Vocals, dry

🔊 Track 7   Vocals, chorus

🔊 Track 8 – Vocals, flanger

🔊 Track 9 – Vocals, phaser

EQ ▶

EQ, or equalization, is an amplitude-based effect. Every DAW has built-in EQ on every track so you can control the levels of high, mid, and low frequencies in your signal. There are a multitude of different EQ plug-ins that can be used for additional EQ processing on your signal as well. EQ is often called an *EQ filter* because it filters the frequencies you hear within the track. EQ impacts the tone of your audio by boosting and cutting frequencies and shaping the sound. There are three basic types of EQ filters: pass, shelf, and parametric.

Amplitude-Based Effects

- *Pass EQ*. A pass EQ cuts extreme frequencies and allows all other frequencies to "pass though." It can exist as a *high-pass filter*, a *low-pass filter*, or both. A low-pass EQ filter cuts high frequencies, allowing the low frequencies to pass through. Likewise, a high-pass EQ filter cuts low frequencies and lets high frequencies through. Pictured below is a low-pass filter.

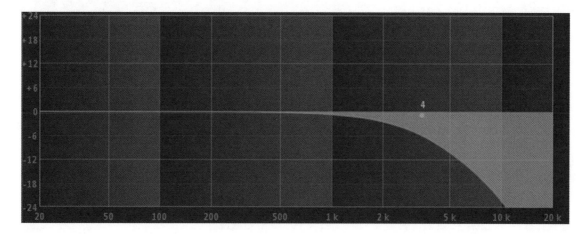

- *Shelf EQ*. Like a pass EQ, this can exist as a *high-shelf*, a *low-shelf,* or both. The main difference is that a shelf takes the frequencies above or below a designated frequency and either boosts or cuts them all. A high-shelf EQ filter used as a cut can sound very similar to a low-pass EQ. The picture below shows a low-shelf EQ boosting frequencies below 200 Hz, and a high-shelf boosting frequencies above 3000 Hz.

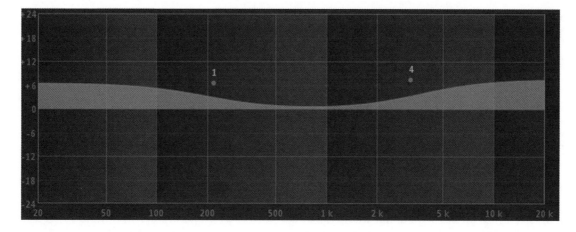

- *Parametric EQ.* This is the most versatile type of EQ because you can boost or cut any frequency, as well as select how wide you want the boost or cut to be. You can home in on a frequency you like and boost it or find a frequency that is displeasing and remove it. The picture below shows two parametric EQ filters: a narrow band boost of 10 dB at 160 Hz and a wider band cut of 6 dB at 4000 Hz.

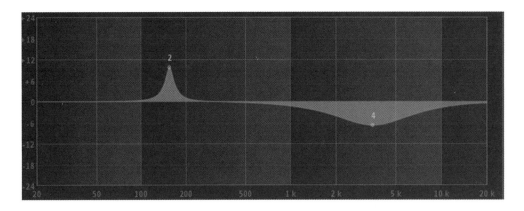

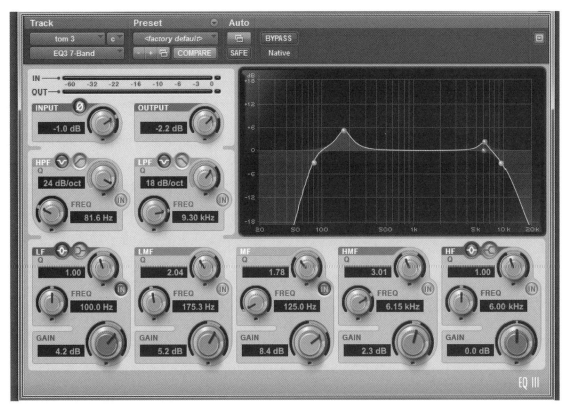

Figure 23

A multi-band EQ utilizing multiple different filters at the same time. Some of the settings shown here are a high-pass filter (cutting the low frequencies below 81 Hz), a parametric EQ (boosting some low-mid frequencies at 175 Hz by 5 dB), another parametric EQ (doing a slight boost at 6 kHz by 2 dB), and a low-pass filter (cutting frequencies above 9.3 kHz).

UNDERSTANDING COMPRESSION

Engineers use *compression* plug-ins to help even out the levels within a recorded track. This is one of the most complex initial concepts to grasp. Most beginners think of volume as the fader level in their mixer and they incorrectly regard compression as turning down a signal. A compressor plug-in is a tool to give you better control over the varying dynamics within a track or group of tracks. By tightening up the dynamic range and squashing down the loudest parts, you can then get more volume out of a track by turning up the whole thing post-compression. This concept of turning a compressed signal back up is called *make-up gain*. It is applied to adjust a signal that has had some of its gain reduced via compression. The end effect of compression paired with make-up gain is that you have turned up only the quiet material on the track, while your loudest material is more consistent in level, with less variation in volume. On a vocal track, this means the whispers and soft consonants can be heard better. But it also means the breaths and pops and background noise are now more noticeable as well. On an acoustic guitar track, it means those big strums are brought more in control, and you will be able to hear the finger picking better. But you may also now hear the performer's soft foot-tapping or breathing.

Many engineers utilize their editing tools to manually turn down (or "duck") breaths and noises that they did not want turned up after compression. Similarly, engineers will often turn down or mute out pops and squeaks that they do not want to hear. Once again, there are no definitively right or wrong answers. Some people really like hearing a performer breathe, as it adds realism, humanity, and intensity to a take. Others prefer a clean track, free of extraneous noises and breaths.

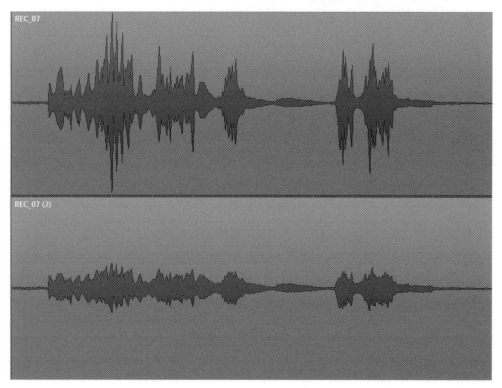

Figure 24
The top track shows a vocal take without any compression. The bottom track shows the same take after compression has been applied. Note how the quiet material was basically unaffected, but the louder material was compressed to be more in line with the volume of the rest of the take. The compressor has decreased the differences between the loud and soft material within the take, allowing for the whole track to be turned up while also maintaining headroom.

Threshold and Ratio

Understanding how the threshold and ratio impact the amount of compression is the key to mastering your compressor plug-ins. The *threshold* is the level above which the compression kicks in. Any audio below the threshold level will not be compressed at all. Once a signal is loud enough to exceed the threshold, it will be compressed. A lower threshold will result in more material being compressed. The *ratio* determines the amount of compression applied to the signal that has exceeded the threshold level. A higher ratio means more compression.

A 1:1 ratio is zero gain reduction. A 2:1 ratio cuts signals above the threshold in half. A 10:1 ratio compresses every signal above the threshold to 1/10. If you have your threshold set at -10 dB and your ratio set at 2:1, this means any signal louder than -10 dB will be compressed by 1 dB for every 2 dB it goes above the threshold.

The *gain reduction* shows how much you are attenuating your signal in decibels.

Multi-Band Compression

Multi-band dynamics plug-ins allow you to set up compressors within specific frequency ranges, dividing up the EQ spectrum and selectively compressing smaller bands of EQ within these smaller ranges. These are powerful plug-ins that can help compress the thumps in a bass without affecting the mid-range in that instrument, or vice versa. You can also use them to help take the harsh "S" and "T" sounds down on a vocal, without compressing the low and low-mid frequencies. Each EQ band is independent and responds to the threshold level it is set for. As such, it can compress both bass frequencies and high-mid frequencies when they are loud. You can choose how much compression to use within each band, and you can also apply make-up gain within each band to help balance out the EQ after the compression is applied. Multi-band compressors are complex but are also great tools to help even out your takes in relative levels within different frequency ranges.

PROducer TIP: Choosing *What* to Compress and *How Much* to Compress

How do you pick what to compress? One simple rule to follow is that when you have loud and quiet parts on the same track, use compression. If you find yourself moving the faders up and down to adjust the volume of a track that includes both quiet and loud parts, a compressor and some make-up gain will help.

Dynamic instruments that I usually compress include vocals, violin, acoustic guitar, mandolin, ukulele, banjo, bass, and clean electric guitars. Anything with distortion on it is already pretty compressed from the overdrive, and thus, typically doesn't need additional compression. Drums are a very dynamic instrument, but trickier. I find compression can sometimes help a drum part that wasn't played evenly, but it can enhance timing mistakes. It can also drain energy out of a drum take because you are reducing the dynamics. Compression can be used to make the drums feel a little wider and all-encompassing. If the drummer is playing inconsistently, compression won't do a whole lot to fix that. For a lively drum sound, a steady drummer who knows when to slam and when to be delicate tends to work *much* better than relying on compression. See what your preferences are as you are working with drums.

Hearing the compression and understanding how much to apply is a skill that takes time and experience to develop. My advice is to use the gain reduction meter within your compressor to gauge how much you are compressing your signal. If you see it is barely registering any reduction and on the loudest parts it only takes off 1 or 2 dB, you are not compressing very much and could probably compress more. If you see it taking 20 dB off of your signal and the noise floor is noticeably loud in the breaks, you are probably compressing too much. A guideline I like to follow when watching the gain reduction meter is to try and shoot for 5–6 dB of compression on the loud parts as a starting point. You can always compress more if needed, but this moderate amount will give you a good level of control over the dynamics without needing to use a ton of make-up gain, which turns up the noise floor. As for make-up gain, first see what your gain reduction meter says you are taking off the signal. Then restore the peak level by boosting your entire track to make up for the gain reduction on the loudest parts. This will give you the best signal for mixing.

CHAPTER 9: MIXING

I like to compare *mixing* to the art of baking a cake. At this point, all our ingredients are chosen and carefully prepared (takes for each instrument and vocal are complete and cleaned up on tracks). Now, as we are approaching the mixing, we need to mix these ingredients in their proper amounts and in the proper order to make the best cake. There are also several decisions we have to make, such as the number of layers, the intensity of flavor, and if we want a thick, moist cake or a dry, fluffy cake. As in any good kitchen, we also have some flavor enhancers and food coloring (effects and plug-ins) at our disposal that we can add as we wish along the way.

Much like taste buds, different people have different musical preferences. Some prefer a simple chocolate cake to an exotic multi-level swirl cake with nuts and fruit. Likewise, some people prefer simple acoustic music with no effects over layers upon layers of musical parts. A mix is what you make of it. But, while there may be no absolute right and wrong, there are techniques that will help you to get better at manipulating a mix and achieve greater clarity of sound.

Figure 25
The mixer window above shows several tracks recorded for a rock song. The slider on the bottom of the window can be moved left and right to access the other tracks that are currently off-screen. You can configure your view within your DAW to show more or less information in the mixer window. Some DAWs will allow you to display multiple mixer windows so you can fit more of your tracks on the screen at the same time.

MIXING BASICS

Below are some basic terms that will help you understand the mixer window. Each track that you have recorded appears as a vertical column in the mixer window. The order of the tracks in your editor is followed here as well. Each track has a set of tools built into the mixer that you can use.

Track Label and Number: the name you have given the track appears at the bottom of each track along with the track number. Using short names allows you to see tracks more easily when you have a full screen in your mixer.

Level: this is a slider that usually starts at *unity volume*, meaning it is playing at the level it was recorded at. Slide the fader up to increase volume and slide it down to decrease volume. At the bottom of the fader, you will see a numerical value showing how much you have turned the track up or down from the unity position.

Panner: this appears either as a left-right slider, or a knob you can turn. Slide or turn it to the left to have the audio on that track sent to the left speaker, and slide or turn it right to have the signal sent to the right speaker. There are many positions in between as well. Use this for spatially positioning elements in your mix.

Mute: the mute button is most commonly shown as a button with a capital "M." When activated by clicking, it will light up and mute all of the contents on that track. Click on it again to unmute that track. You can mute multiple tracks at the same time.

Solo: this is usually labeled with a capital "S." When you click on it, the contents of that track get soloed out, muting all other tracks. This is handy to use when checking fades, cross-fades, finding noises, and checking the EQ on a given track. You can also use the tool to hear select combinations of tracks in your mix, segregated from everything else.

Meters: the meters will display the levels you are outputting from each track. Note how tracks with panning show up differently on the meters. You can set your DAW to hold the peaks or not. Holding the peaks is handy when you want to see the loudest point on any track. At the bottom of the meter is a numerical value that shows the current volume of the audio being played on that track.

Record Arm: the button with the small circle in it arms the track for recording. In most DAWs, it will light up red when the track is armed for recording. Most engineers arm and disarm tracks within the editor window because this is visually easier when recording new takes. But you can also arm tracks within the mixer window, or see which tracks are armed in either window. After arming a track, clicking on the record button will record and capture whatever is coming into the designated input. You can record to multiple tracks at the same time. Remember to disarm tracks when you are finished to avoid accidentally recording extra takes when you move on.

Automation: the "W" and "R" buttons are for "writing" and "reading" automation. They are used when you want to make changes within the mix, like turning up a small section of a track and then turning it back down. Automation can be used for almost any parameter. Click on "W" to "write," or capture, your automation. The DAW will capture and remember all the changes made on that track, from levels and pans to EQ and the mix on your effects. It'll also remember *when* you made those changes. Click "W" again to stop writing automation data. Click on "R" to then read that data and see those changes take place in real time while listening back. You might use automation for level adjustments within a track, mutes, pan sweeps, EQ changes or sweeps, boosting or cutting an effect, and changing the parameters within an effect (such as taking a short reverb and lengthening it for a specific drum hit).

Additional Features: the following features are seen on each track in some DAWs. The button labeled "L" turns up a track by a predetermined amount, allowing you to hear details better. Use it when you are thinking, "What is this track playing right now and how is it fitting into the mix?" The button labeled "E" (or "e") will bring up a window for that channel's settings known as the *channel strip*, where you can apply EQ and add inserts or auxiliary (aux) effects. Some DAWs will open this editor window when you double-click on a track, and others will allow you to open individual effects or EQs by clicking on that part of the channel in the mixer or editor window. Use these channel settings to add processing or effects, or to change the EQ.

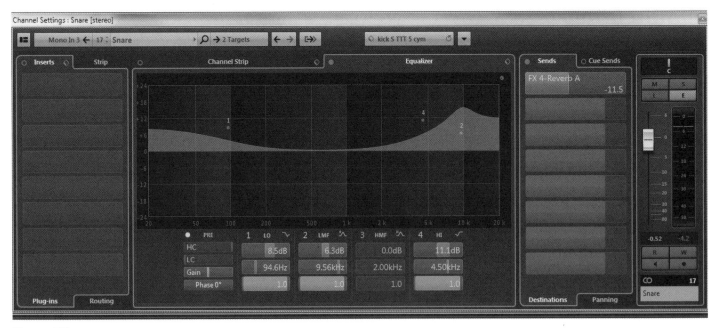

Figure 26
The expanded channel settings for a snare track, often called a channel strip. This is brought up by clicking the "e" on a channel in either the mixer or the editor window. You can see there are currently no plug-ins in the insert section on the left. Three of the five EQs are being used to add high and low frequencies to this snare, and an auxiliary send is being used to send some of this snare signal to a reverb channel that has been set up in the auxiliary effects of the mixer.

While it's tempting to dive in and start putting effects on tracks and leveling out the various components of your mix, I recommend you first take a little time to: 1) make sure your takes have been cleaned up in the editor, and 2) organize your mixer. Like baking a cake, an organized and clean kitchen is much easier to work in, so I always recommend cleaning and organizing things at the start of mixing.

- Clean Your Tracks. Double-check that you have included cross-fades where needed, and make sure there are fades on the starts and ends of your takes. If you have layers upon layers of takes, I strongly recommend you clean those up and keep only the takes you intend to use. Otherwise, you might have problems later when things shift and you can't find your favorite take. Clean up timings as needed. Remove long sections of silence where the performance takes a break. Noise will add up between multiple tracks if you allow it; once you start mixing and using compression, that noise will just multiply. Do yourself the favor of cleaning up your tracks and takes before tackling the mix.

- Organize Your Mixer. Put the tracks in an order that makes sense to you. I like to put all of the guitar parts in one section of the mixer, all of the keyboard parts together, and then continue with drums and percussion, vocals, etc. This will make it much easier to mix similar parts together and adjust settings within the groups. Rename tracks if it is helpful (e.g., "Guitar 1," "Guitar 2," and "Guitar 3" could be renamed "Rhythm Gtr Left," "Rhythm Gtr Right," and "Gtr leads and solo" to make it easier to find and adjust things later). I like to put my sub-group tracks right next to the individual tracks that make up that sub-group, so I can find them and work seamlessly between them on the mixer. I also like to put all of my effect tracks in the same spot on the right of my mixer. That way, I know where to find them during the mix when I want to make adjustments.

MIXING THE RHYTHM SECTION

You may find it useful to mute out all vocals and leads in your mix and start with the rhythm section first. Start with the drums and work on panning and EQ for each drum microphone. Remember, drums bleed a lot between microphones, so your EQ will only be as powerful as the microphone is in your overall drum mix. Once you have a solid drum sound, add in the bass and any percussion instruments. Compare the bass frequencies in the kick drum with the bass frequencies in the bass guitar or key bass. Make sure you can hear them both and that one isn't masking the low-end frequencies from the other. Many engineers like to add brightness to drums, especially cymbals and overhead microphones. This added shimmer can be heard on most modern recordings, giving clarity to the drums and brightening the whole sound.

SUBTRACTIVE MIXING

One big thing to keep in mind is not only, "Should we be adding to the mix?" but, "Could we be subtracting?" You can often solve problems by turning things down, or employing *subtractive EQ*. If you find that you keep turning things up so you can hear them, consider "what is keeping me from hearing this part?" and then turn that element down. Often, a frequency range from one instrument can get in the way of hearing a different instrument. For example, if you have a warm-sounding guitar part, the bass track and kick drum combined with the left hand of the organ or piano may be masking the guitar so it cannot be easily heard. Thinking of it from a subtractive standpoint, rolling off some low-mid frequencies on the organ or piano part will create a hole for the warm guitar to appear as well. Also, a cut to the low-mid frequencies on the bass around 200 Hz may open a pocket where the guitar can come through more without even adjusting any fader levels on your mixer. There may well be some additive solutions. For example, adding some high frequencies to the guitar will help. You could also turn up the warm guitar so it takes up more of the sonic landscape.

MAKING SPACE USING EQ AND PANNING

As mentioned earlier with EQ, every instrument and part in your mix has a frequency range to it. For a violin, this includes mid and high frequencies. For a bass, it is mostly low and low-mid frequencies. Understanding the frequency ranges for different instruments and parts will allow you to give each component its space within the frequency spectrum. Combining these ranges within your frequency range with special panning will give you optimal clarity. By shaping the EQs and pans on your tracks so every part has its place, you are creating a multi-leveled mix, where each component is given room to be heard within the bigger picture.

Listen to the partial mix of "Never Let You Go" by Smith & Jackson. Note how the guitars are panned and how the hi-hats are spread wide between both ears. The horn mix is tilted to the left so it doesn't compete with the steady rhythm guitar on the right, or the chorus vocals. The lead vocal is center-panned with a nice stereo reverb on it. When the chorus enters, the backing vocals are spread out to both ears, with stereo doubles of each part. This means the backing vocals and harmonies are balanced between the ears but aren't competing with the lead vocal for space. Each component has its own place and can be heard clearly as a result of the panning. Plus, the mix is more intriguing to listen to because of the spatial positioning of the tracks.

 Track 10 – "Never Let You Go" Mix

INSTRUMENT FREQUENCY RANGES

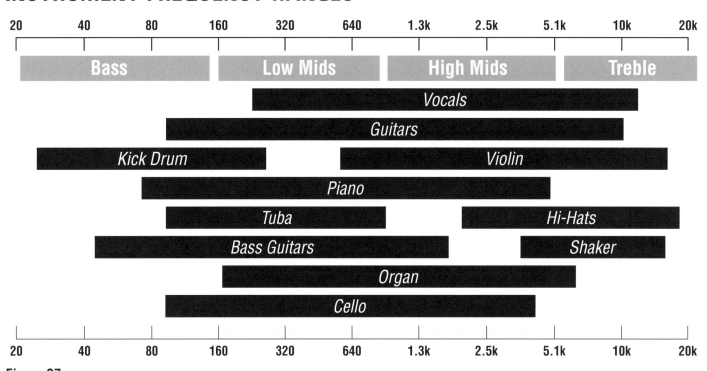

Figure 27
The human hearing spectrum of 20 Hz to 20 kHz, approximate fundamental frequency ranges of various instruments, and how they relate.

Let's again use the analogy of baking a cake to illustrate this point. We have cherries, lemons, and raspberries (three different instruments) that we want to include in our three-layered cake. If we put all three fruits into all three layers, it may be hard to pick out those flavors in your finished product. However, if we make three cake layers and use one fruit in each, it will be much easier to taste the individual fruits within the finished cake. Another option may be to use the cherries in the cake batter, use the raspberries to make a jam that goes between the layers, and use the lemon in the frosting. This will keep the individual fruit flavors separate and make for a more interesting cake. In doing this, we can achieve a truly combined mix where the individual strength of each component makes the whole mix stronger. Maintaining the individual identity of each fruit will also help to further enhance the flavor of the others.

Applying this to different instruments, when do you want each instrument to be noticed? Where in the stereo field and in the EQ range does this instrument fit in with the others? Where do they overlap and how can we separate them appropriately and artistically?

CREATING DEPTH WITH EQ AND EFFECTS

Engineers tend to refer to instruments with a lot of low frequencies as "dark" or "boomy," and those with prominent high frequencies as "bright" or "shimmery." Instruments and performances vary from loud to soft, fast to slow, transient to sustained, and high to low. Your job as a mixing engineer is to take all of these variables and transform them into a single cohesive idea that people want to listen to. A good mix starts with a well-written song, containing good takes delivered by talented people that are put together with solid editing. The mixing engineer needs to consider musical style, mood, energy fluctuations, emotional variations, and the instruments and tools at their disposal. As much as mixing can be technical, it is also an art. Like any art, it is subjective.

A great way to communicate energy and forward motion in a mix is through variation. Varying EQ within a take, or varying the effect usage, can be a great way to "take away" and "add back in" as previously recommended. Be bold and then back off if needed. Experiment with using drastic EQs and effects only in certain parts of the song. Try taking out instruments for some sections and experiment with panning changes in transitions. These are all spices and seasonings at your disposal to use within your evolving mixes.

LISTEN, ADJUST, AND LISTEN AGAIN

Many engineers like to listen to their mixes in different environments. Listen on speakers, then on headphones. Listen at home, in your car, and through your laptop speakers. See how your ideas translate in these different listening environments and adjust accordingly.

Keep some notes and make changes to your mix, saving it as a new version each time so that you can go back to earlier versions if needed. Think about each instrument and component. Ask yourself, one by one, if you like how they sound in the mix. Listen to the mid, low, and high frequencies, assessing if there is a good balance. Force yourself to think from a subtractive standpoint and listen for elements, or EQ ranges within those elements, to pull down. If you find you are getting fatigued or frustrated, give your ears a rest and come back to it later. With fresh ears, you will hear things differently.

PROducer TIP: Be Flexible and Open to Critique—Seek Out Help

Undoubtedly, you will get better at mixing over time. One of my most important bits of advice is to be open to ideas, flexible to change, and willing to experiment. Stubbornness is the enemy of a good mix. Be willing to try something different even if you have invested hours on another idea. Occasionally, you will need to take a step back so you can make two steps forward. Such a mindset will allow you to improve and learn new tricks and techniques for future mixes. Ask others for their opinions and be open to feedback.

For your first several mixes, I always recommend hiring a professional to listen and provide constructive and specific advice. You will learn so much by getting an honest, professional opinion from someone with years of experience. For a small investment, you'll receive an invaluable return. You will also be adding tools to your mixing toolbox for future projects. Your family and friends are good options to run your mixes by, but they may be afraid to give you criticism or may not be able to give you usable audio advice. If you are truly open to ideas and critique, you will never regret seeking professional feedback on your mixes. You'll grow and improve your mixing skills and, along the way, your confidence in making better mixing decisions.

CHAPTER 10: MASTERING

WHAT IS MASTERING?

Mastering begins with your mix. A mix is a single stereo file containing the combination of audio that you applied during your mixing process. Going back to the baking analogy, you now have a bowl full of batter that has all of the ingredients in the proportions you want. *Mastering* is taking that mix and baking it at the correct temperature for the right amount of time to get a perfect cake.

Audio mastering is often a misunderstood process. Essentially, it involves comparing your mix against other songs in that genre, balancing out overall EQ on the mix, and making the entire mix louder. This last part is done so that no one will need to adjust the volume, bass, or treble on their system between songs if yours was one part of a mixed playlist. Mastering is making your song ready for distribution by bringing it up to commonly accepted EQ balances, dynamic ranges, and overall levels.

To properly master a song, you need to compare and analyze the mix at different points, hearing which frequencies might need to be cut and which frequencies might need to be boosted to help even out the overall EQ on the song. For example, let's say I have a mix with the perfect blend between the instruments and components. But overall, I think it's a little low-end heavy in comparison with other songs on the album, something caused by the specific instrumentation of bass guitar, kick drum, and organ (which all lie at the bottom end of the EQ spectrum). In this case, I'd apply a shelf EQ to cut a bit of that low-frequency range, bringing the overall mix to a more balanced EQ. Note how applying this shelf EQ impacts the entire mix. This low-end shelf cut gets rolled off of everything, including guitars, bass, kick drum, organ, and any other component containing low frequencies. In other words, I can't just take bass frequencies out of the bass guitar. This would be like trying to take sugar or food coloring out of the cake batter after it has all been mixed together. This is important. Mastering can't fix a bad mix. But it can certainly enhance a good mix.

Listen to the following audio tracks to hear a completed mix before and after mastering.

 Track 11 – "Never Let You Go" Unmastered

 Track 12 – "Never Let You Go" Mastered

Comparing these two audio tracks, note not only the obvious level differences, but also the level of control over the low-end frequencies in the mastered mix compared to the unmastered mix. Also, hear how the mastered mix has a boosted and compressed high end, giving it a bright (but not overly bright) shimmer. Recognizing these improvements reinforces the value of both the mastering process and a good mastering engineer.

CHAIN OF FILTERS AND DYNAMICS PROCESSING

Technically speaking, mastering usually involves EQ and dynamics filters. In some cases, it might also involve noise reduction and application of effects prior to these filters. Here is a basic mastering chain of effects for a song that has a good mix and does not need noise reduction.

1. *Multi-Band EQ.* A wide EQ featuring many EQs within it, including multiple parametric EQs, along with shelf- and pass-filter options.

2. *Multi-Band Dynamics Processing.* A multi-band compressor with which you can compress different ranges separately from each other.

3. *Limiter.* A high-ratio compressor designed to maximize the volume of your mix. This limits the maximum volume of the loud peaks, applying compression where they approach digital zero and allowing a nice, loud result without clipping.

ADJUSTING YOUR MIX IN RESPONSE TO THE MASTERING

You might find that the mastering process shines new light on your mix, which inspires you to make retrospective adjustments. If you are able to do so, go back into your mix, make those adjustments, and *render*, or save out a new mix file (aka, "bounce"). Then you can apply the same mastering settings and see what it sounds like in the finished product. This is a common occurrence nowadays and can be a great way to perfect your mixes.

PROducer TIP: Preview Your Mix With Some Mastering Plug-Ins

I like to set up a few basic plug-ins in the inserts on my main output bus while I am mixing. I often will use a multi-band compressor to help control the overall EQ balance, using four bands of compression to squash sections where frequencies might be overly represented within a certain range of the EQ spectrum. I also like to use a limiter after any compression, so I can crank up the output level. This means I can preview the mix at a hot level while avoiding clipping. By simply adding these two plug-ins into my main bus, I can now hear what the mix sounds like with some basic mastering applied.

Before I bounce out the mix, I always make sure my multi-band is only subtly compressing any given band. I also bring the limiter gain down, so I have appropriate headroom in the mix. This allows me to hear the mix in the context of mastering, before the mastering process begins. It can help to avoid wasting time going back and forth between mixing and mastering adjustments.

FINALIZING YOUR MASTERED MIX

After you have compared your mastered mix against others and have applied the chain of mastering effects and filters, you will need to save the mastered mix as a new file. This way, you can always go back to the unmastered mix if you want to make mastering adjustments later. Then, save the new mastered mix as both a full-quality lossless file (wav or aif) and an mp3 file. When saving your mp3 file, you can include *metadata*, which is information stored within the digital file (including song name, artist name, album name, copyright information, genre, and many other optional bits of information).

PROducer TIP: Quality Matters!

Always record and mix using lossless files and then convert to mp3 files after all audio work has been completed. This will give you the best results, allowing for smaller, easily downloadable files for the end product. When you encode an mp3 of your final mastered mix, try using settings for 192 kbps or 256 kbps rather than the common, low-quality 128 kbps. This will give you crisp, full mixes that can still be transferred easily and quickly.

RECORDING & MUSIC TECHNOLOGY BOOKS

101 RECORDING TIPS
STUFF ALL THE PROS KNOW AND USE

by Adam St. James

Tips, suggestions, advice and other useful information garnered through a lifetime of home and pro studio recording adventures are presented in this book, which includes dozens of entries learned firsthand from legendary producers, engineers, and artists.

00311035 Book/CD Pack............$14.95

AUDIO ENGINEERING FOR SOUND REINFORCEMENT
by John Eargle and Chris Foreman
JBL Pro Audio

All aspects of speech and music sound reinforcement are covered comprehensively in this book. It includes sections on: fundamentals for audio engineers; classes of hardware engineers will use; the basics of system design; and individual design areas.

00650509 ....$49.95

THE DIY GUIDE TO MAKING MUSIC VIDEOS
FOR THE INDEPENDENT MUSICIAN

by Jon Forsyth

This guide is written for the DIY crowd. It will prepare you to get results that are as professional as possible without the accompanying budget.

00283387 Book/Online Video $19.99

FIRST 50 RECORDING TECHNIQUES YOU SHOULD KNOW TO TRACK MUSIC
by Bill Gibson

This collection of modern, easy-to-understand techniques for recording music in a variety of settings provides tools and information to help you capture high-quality sounds on par with those recorded by seasoned professionals.

00294443 ....$14.99

GUERILLA HOME RECORDING
HOW TO GET GREAT SOUND FROM ANY STUDIO
Music Pro Guides Series

by Karl Coryat

This trusted guide includes chapters devoted to instrument recording, humanizing drum patterns, mixing with plug-ins and virtual consoles, and a new section on using digital audio skills.

00331940 ....$24.99

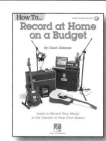

HOW TO RECORD AT HOME ON A BUDGET
LEARN TO REOCRD YOUR MUSIC IN THE COMFORT OF YOUR OWN HOME!

by Chad Johnson

Examine all aspects of getting quality recordings from your modest home studio rig with this accessible book.

00131211 Book/Online Audio.....................$17.99

MASTERING EXPLAINED
by Michael Costa & Chad Johnson

This book sheds light on how to apply mastering techniques in the following areas: mastering stereo mixes and stems • fixing problematic mixes • equalization, compression, limiting and dither • mid/side processing • and more.

00298789 Book/Online Video $14.99

MIXING & MASTERING
HAL LEONARD RECORDING METHOD

by Bill Gibson

Techniques and procedures that result in a polished mix and powerful master recording are demonstrated in this book, using current plug-ins, software, and hardware. You'll then learn how to prepare the mastered recording for CD replication, streaming, or download.

00333254 Book/Online Media + DVD-ROM $39.99

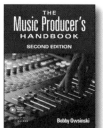

THE MUSIC PRODUCER'S HANDBOOK
SECOND EDITION
Music Pro Guides

by Bobby Owsinski

Chapters on self-production, small studio production, and how the new songwriter-producer and engineer-producer hybrids make money in our new digital music world are included in this valuable recource book for producers.

00151139 Book/Online Media $34.99

HAL•LEONARD®

Order these and many more publications from your favorite music retailer at

halleonard.com

POWER TOOLS FOR SYNTHESIZER PROGRAMMING
THE ULTIMATE REFERENCE FOR SOUND DESIGN

by Jim Aikin

Even if you're just grabbing presets to play on the keyboard, you'll get to the music faster thanks to the tips in this book. Chapters on oscillators, filters, envelope generators, LFOs, effects, and digital audio are included.

00131064 Book/Online Media $29.99

Q ON PRODUCING
THE SOUL AND SCIENCE OF MASTERING MUSIC AND WORK

by Quincy Jones with Bill Gibson

Quincy's observations, culled from over a year of in-depth interviews, are collected and presented in this book and accompanying DVD-ROM, providing an unparalleled course of instruction from one of the true legends of American music.

00332755 Hardcover Book/DVD Pack $34.99

SOUND REINFORCEMENT HANDBOOK
by Gary Davis & Ralph Jones
Yamaha

This unique and comprehensive book covers all aspects of designing and using audio amplification systems for public address and musical performance. It features information on both the audio theory involved and practical applications.

00500964 ....$34.95

STUFF GOOD SYNTH PLAYERS SHOULD KNOW
AN A TO Z GUIDE TO GETTING BETTER

by Mark Harrison

Take your playing from ordinary to extraordinary with this all-encompassing book/CD pack for synthesizer players. You'll receive tips on techniques to help your programming and performances become more professional.

00311773 Book/CD Pack.....................$19.99

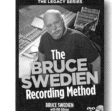

THE BRUCE SWEDIEN RECORDING METHOD
THE LEGACY SERIES

by Bruce Swedien & Bill Gibson

Bruce Swedien explains many of the techniques he has used to get award-winning drum, bass, guitar, keyboard, vocal, string, and brass sounds in this book. This resource is perfect for anyone interested in mixing the best possible music recordings.

00333302 Book/DVD-ROM Pack.....................$39.99

Prices, contents, and availability subject to change without notice.